D0982706

The Scarecrow Author Bibliographies

An Index to
Arthur Miller Criticism

Second Edition

by

Tetsumaro Hayashi

The Scarecrow Author Bibliographies, No. 3

The Scarecrow Press, Inc.

Metuchen, N.J.   1976

Library of Congress Cataloging in Publication Data

Hayashi, Tetsumaro.
    An index to Arthur Miller criticism.

    First ed. published under title: Arthur Miller
criticism, 1930-1967.
    Includes index.
    1. Miller, Arthur, 1915-   --Bibliography. I. Ti-
tle.
Z8574.88.H37 1976   [PS3525.I5156]   016.812'5'2
ISBN 0-8108-0947-8   76-10293

TO
AKIKO AND RICHARD HIDEKI HAYASHI
WITH LOVE

CONTENTS

PREFACE AND ACKNOWLEDGMENTS

When asked by my publisher whether or not I wished to revise and update my Arthur Miller Criticism (1930-1967), published in 1969, I had mixed feelings about accepting that difficult responsibility; first, because I am not a specialist in Arthur Miller studies; secondly, because such a comprehensive bibliography would inevitably invite the exacting criticism of learned scholars who might traditionally bear biases or perhaps contempt for a bibliographer; thirdly, because I know that a bibliography of this kind is necessarily a labor of love, a risky and often thankless job, demanding a great deal while giving little more than personal satisfaction in return; and lastly, because, I had, as always, several important editorial and research projects to direct at that time.

In spite of these difficulties and hesitations, I finally decided to accept the challenge for several reasons. First, I felt obligated to provide a revised and updated bibliography for the general public, and especially for reference librarians, students, and teachers who have patiently used the older bibliography in spite of its limitations and imperfections. Secondly, I wanted to make this book more functional by drastically simplifying the organization. Lastly, no Arthur Miller specialist has, to my knowledge, provided a book-length bibliography in the period since my own bibliography was published in 1969.

Here, I have attempted to compile a more functional and useful bibliography to save students, teachers, reference librarians, and scholars time, energy, and frustration by putting as many known bibliographical sources under one roof, the roof itself better organized than in 1969. As I recall, the 1969 volume, despite its shortcomings, received about ten favorable reviews, most of which were written by reference librarians and experts who knew the value of a comprehensive, though not exhaustive, bibliography. In addition, the book precipitated at least one harsh review from which I learned a great deal (although nothing about courtesy or scholarly decorum).

vii

Apart from this it was simply time for a revised, enlarged, and updated bibliography, and so I made the following improvements and revisions: 1) simplification of the structure of the bibliography by avoiding unnecessary repetitions, preparing a more extensive Index (keyed to serialized entry numbers to speed up use), adding unpublished master's theses, and separately listing Arthur Miller's interviews; 2) clarification of both old and new items; and 3) a more detailed and accurate chronology of Arthur Miller. As the title of the book indicates, I have stressed the secondary sources. In this book I tried to include only English language materials published through 1974. If I have failed to include something of importance, or have documented an entry improperly, I would ask the user of this bibliography to inform me of it.

While compiling this book, I accumulated a debt of gratitude to a number of people and institutions, most of whom are listed below or in the Appendices. To those omitted through oversight, I acknowledge a great debt. Dr. Reloy Garcia, Professor of English at Creighton University, assisted me in the overall project and offered me advice and wisdom. Professor Donald L. Siefker, Head of the Information Service of the Ball State University Library, assisted me on reference questions and advised me on the project whenever possible. All the book-length studies on Arthur Miller and a number of standard and specialized reference guides provided me with important sources to be indexed in this book. Such publishers as David McKay, Prentice-Hall, Twayne, Frederick Ungar, Viking Press, and others helped me with my bibliographical research by either giving or lending me their latest books on Arthur Miller for examination. Mr. John R. Payne, Associate Librarian of the Humanities Research Center Library at the University of Texas in Austin; Mr. Donald W. Fowle, Theater Collection Librarian of the New York Public Library; and Miss Harriet C. Jameson, Head of the Department of Rare Books and Special Collections, and Mrs. Margaret Berg, Manuscript Cataloger, both of the University of Michigan Libraries in Ann Arbor, helped me update their holdings of Miller's unpublished manuscripts.

It is to these authors, editors, compilers, scholars, librarians, publishers, bibliographers, specialists, and friends that I owe my profound gratitude.

Tetsumaro Hayashi

Ball State University
Muncie, Indiana
September 1, 1975

KEY TO ABBREVIATIONS

A	Autographed
ALS	Autographed letter, signed.
AM	Arthur Miller.
AMS	Autographed manuscript.
ANS	Autographed note, signed.
AP	Autographed postcard.
CAAS Bulletin	Canadian Association for American Studies Bulletin.
DA	Dissertation Abstracts.
DAI	Dissertation Abstracts International.
(FR)	Film review.
Illus. (or illus.)	Illustrator or illustrated by.
Inc.	Incomplete.
M	Miller.
Misc.	Miscellaneous.
MS	Manuscript.
N & Q	Notes and Queries.
N. B.	Nota bene, note well or take notice
[n. d.]	no date identified or known.
[n. v.]	no volume number identified.
pp.	pages.
(R)	Review.
Rep.	Reprinted.
S	Signed.
T	Typed.
T/cc	Typed copies.
TLS	Typed letter, signed.
TMS	Typed manuscript.
t. p.	title page.
Tr. (or tr.)	Translator or translated by.

CHRONOLOGY OF ARTHUR MILLER

1915   October 17: Born on 112th Street in Harlem, New York City, the son of Isadore and Augusta (Barnett) Miller.

1929   Family moved to Brooklyn, N. Y.

1932   Graduated from the Abraham Lincoln High School in Brooklyn.

1934-38   Enrolled in journalism at the University of Michigan.

1936   Honors at Dawn, first play, produced at the University of Michigan. Won University's Avery Hopwood Award.
Won the Theatre Guild National Award for The Grass Still Grows.

1938   No Villain, revised and entitled They Too Arise, produced at the University of Michigan. Won another Hopwood Award and a prize of the Theatre Guild Bureau of New Plays.
Received the B. A. degree from the University of Michigan.

1938-43   Returned to New York and worked at various jobs. Wrote scripts for Federal Theatre projects, Columbia Workshop (CBS), and Cavalcade of America (NBC).

1940   Married Mary Grace Slattery, whom he had met at college (divorced in 1956).

1944   Toured army camps collecting background material for a screenplay, The Story of G. I. Joe, based on Pyle's book, Here Is Your War. A diary M. kept while visiting Army camps in the United

States, researching for a film, The Story of G. I.
Joe, the war life of journalist Ernie Pyle, was
published under the title, Situation Normal.
November: The Man Who Had All the Luck, his
first Broadway play, published and produced on
Broadway.
Received the Theatre Guild National Award.

1945   Focus, a novel about anti-Semitism, published.
        The Story of G. I. Joe, a film, released.
        Published That They May Win (one-act) in The
        Best One-Act Plays of 1944, ed. Margaret May-
        orga (New York: Dodd, Mead, 1945), pp. 45-60.

1947   All My Sons produced, published, and won New
        York Drama Critics' Circle Award, and the Don-
        aldson Award.

1948   Film version of All My Sons produced.

1949   Death of a Salesman produced, published, and won
        American Theatre Wing Award for the play.
        Antoinette Perry Award.
        Billboard's Donaldson Award (July).
        Jewish Writers, Artists and Scientists American
        Committee Award (June).
        Named one of ten "outstanding fathers" by the Na-
        tional Father's Day Committee (see New York
        Times, May 27, 1949, p. 5:3).
        New York Drama Critics' Circle Award for the
        play.
        New York Newspaper Guild Page One Award for
        the play (March).
        Pulitzer Prize for the play.
        Theatre Club Award for the play (April).

1950   An Enemy of the People, M's adaptation of Ibsen's
        play, produced.

1951   An Enemy of the People, an adaptation from Ib-
        sen's play, published.
        Film version of Death of a Salesman produced.

1953   The Crucible published.
        Won the Antoinette Perry Award for The Crucible.

1954   Won the National Association of Independent Schools
        Award for The Crucible (Viking Press).

Denied passport to visit Brussels by State Department.

1955 A Memory of Two Mondays and the one-act version of A View from the Bridge produced.
A View from the Bridge published.
Won the New York Drama Critics' Circle Award for A View.

1956 Divorced from his wife, the former Mary Grace Slattery (see New York Times, June 2, 1956, p. 24:6).
June 16: Received his Honorary Doctor's Degree at the University of Michigan (see New York Times, June 17, 1956, p. 8:1).
June 29: Married Marilyn Monroe (divorced in 1961).
The revised two-act version of A View from the Bridge produced in London.

1957 Collected Plays published.
Convicted of contempt of Congress after trial, fined $500 and given a suspended 30-day jail sentence.

1958 The conviction was reversed on appeal to the U. S. Court of Appeals for the District of Columbia.
Elected to the National Institute of Arts and Letters.
Film version of The Crucible produced in France.

1959 Won the American Academy of Arts and Letters Gold Medal Award.

1960 Final separation from his second wife Marilyn Monroe.

1961 The Misfits, a film script, written, produced, and released.
March 7: His mother died of a heart ailment at the age of 70 (Mrs. Augusta Miller, wife of Isadore Miller, a salesman; see New York Times, March 7, 1961, p. 35:3).
The Crucible was turned into an opera by Robert Ward.
Roberto Rossellini presented an operatic version of A View from the Bridge in Italy.
Divorced Marilyn Monroe (see New York Times,

Jan. 25, 1961, p. 35:4).

1962	Film version of A View from the Bridge. Married Ingeborg Morath. Daughter Rebecca born. Marilyn Monroe died.
1964	After the Fall published and produced at the Repertory Theatre of Lincoln Center. Incident at Vichy produced in December at the Repertory Theatre of Lincoln Center
1965	Elected president of the P.E.N., an international literary organization (until 1969). Incident at Vichy published.
1966	Television production of Death of a Salesman.
1967	I Don't Need You Any More, a collection of short stories published.
1968	The Price published.
1969-70	Won the Brandeis University Creative Arts Award.
1971	The Creation of the World and Other Business produced; The Portable AM, ed. Harold Clurman, published.
1972	The Creation of the World and Other Business published.
1973	Won the Albert Einstein Commemorative Award.

Cf.: 1) Clurman (1971); 2) Corrigan (1969); 3) Current Biography (1973); 4) Encyclopaedia Britannica (1974-75); 5) Hayashi (1969); 6) Hayman (1970); 7) Moss (1967); and 8) Weales 1967).

PART I:
PRIMARY SOURCES
(PUBLISHED WORKS BY ARTHUR MILLER)

I. PLAYS AND RADIO SCRIPTS

[For the latest available editions, consult the latest Books in Print and Paperbound Books in Print.]

1. After the Fall. New York: Viking, 1964.

2. All My Sons. New York: Reynal & Hitchcock, 1947. New York: Dramatists Play Service, 1947.

3. Collected Plays. New York: Viking, 1957.
   Contents: All My Sons, Death of a Salesman, The Crucible, A View from the Bridge (in revised version), A Memory of Two Mondays, along with a 50-page introduction.

4. The Creation of the World and Other Business. New York: Viking, 1973.
   "AM Writes on God and Man, Good and Evil" (Excerpts from The Creation of the World and Other Business). Vogue, 161 (January 1973), 132-33.

5. The Crucible. New York. Viking, 1953.

6. Death of a Salesman. New York: Viking, 1949.

7. An Enemy of the People. New York: Viking, 1951 (Adaptation of Henrik Ibsen's play).

8. "Fame," Yale Literary Magazine, 140 (March 1971), 32-40.

9. Grandpa and the Statue, in Radio Drama in Action, ed. Erik Barnouw. New York: Farrar and Rinehart, 1947, pp. 267-81.

10. The Guardsman by Ferenc Molnar, adapted by Miller, in Theatre Guild on the Air, ed. H. William Fitelson. New York: Rinehart, 1947, pp. 65-98; trans. Grace I. Colbron and Hans Bartsch (original play copyrighted

by Hans Bartsch in 1924).

11. Incident at Vichy. New York: Viking, 1965.

12. The Man Who Had All the Luck in Cross-Section: A
     Collection of New American Writing, ed. Edwin Seaver.
     New York: L. B. Fischer, 1944, pp. 486-552 (a pre-
     production of the play).

13. A Memory of Two Mondays. New York: Viking, 1955
     (with A View from the Bridge).

14. The Misfits. New York: Dell, 1961 (comprising film-
     script in novel form, with original short story of the
     same title).

15. The Portable AM, ed. Harold Clurman. New York:
     Viking, 1971.
          Contents: Biographical Notes, vii. Editor's Intro-
     duction, xi. I. Plays. Death of a Salesman, The
     Crucible, Incident at Vichy, The Price. II. Other
     Works. The Misfits [I] (the original story), From
     The Misfits [II] (a cinema novel), "Fame" (a story),
     "Fitter's Night" (a story), From In Russia, Lines
     from "California" (a poem). Bibliography of Works
     by Arthur Miller.

16. The Price. New York: Viking, 1968.

17. The Pussycat and the Expert Plumber Who Was a Man,
     in One Hundred Non-Royalty Radio Plays, ed. William
     Kozlenko. New York: Greenberg, 1941, pp. 20-30.

18. The Story of Gus, in Radio's Best Plays, ed. Joseph
     Liss. New York: Greenberg, 1947, pp. 303-19.

19. That They May Win (1943), in The Best One-Act Plays
     of 1944, ed. Margaret Mayorga. New York: Dodd,
     Mead, 1945, pp. 45-59.

20. A View from the Bridge. New York: Viking, 1955
     (with A Memory of Two Mondays).

21. William Ireland's Confession, in One Hundred Non-Roy-
     alty Radio Plays, compiled by William Kozlenko. New
     York: Greenberg, 1941, pp. 512-21.

2. FICTION (NOVELS AND SHORT STORIES)

[For the latest available novels and short story anthologies, check the latest Books in Print.]

22. "Fame." See "The Recognitions."

23. "Fitter's Night," in I Don't Need You Any More; Stories. New York: Viking Press, 1966, pp. 175-223; The Portable AM, ed. Harold Clurman. New York: Viking, 1971, pp. 503-49.

24. Focus. New York: Reynal and Hitchcock, 1945.

25. "Glimpse at a Jockey," Story, 5(1962), 130-140. Also in The Noble Savage, No. 5. Cleveland: World, 1962, pp. 138-40; and AM's I Don't Need You Any More, pp. 114-17.

26. I Don't Need You Any More; Stories. New York: Viking Press, 1951.
      Contents. Foreword about Distances, "I Don't Need You Any More," "Monte Sant' Angel," "Please Don't Kill Anything," "The Misfits," "Glimpse at a Jockey," "The Prophecy," "Fitter's Night," "A Search for a Future."

27. "I Don't Need You Any More," Esquire, 52 (December 1959), 270-309; also in AM's I Don't Need You Any More, pp. 3-52.

28. "It Takes a Thief," Collier's, 112 (February 8, 1947), 23, 75-6.

29. Jane's Blanket, illus. Emily A. McCully. New York: Viking Press, 1963 (children's story for ages 4-6).

30. The Misfits (1960). New York: Viking, 1961.

31. "The Misfits," Esquire, 50 (October 1957), 158-66; al-
     so AM's I Don't Need You Any More, pp. 79-113; and
     The Portable AM, ed. Harold Clurman, pp. 494-80.

32. "Monte Sant' Angelo," Harper's, 202 (March 1951), 39-
     47. Reprinted in Prize Stories of 1951, ed. Herschel
     Brickell. New York: Doubleday, 1951; also AM's I
     Don't Need You Any More, pp. 53-70.

33. "Please Don't Kill Anything," Story, 1(1960), 126-31.
     Also The Noble Savage, No. 1. Cleveland: World Pub-
     lishing Co., 1960, pp. 126-31. Also printed in Redbook,
     117 (October 1961), 48-49; and AM's I Don't Need You
     Any More, pp. 71-78.

34. "The Prophecy," Esquire, 56 (December 1961), 140-41,
     286-87; and AM's I Don't Need You Any More, pp. 118-
     66.

35. "Recognitions," Esquire, 66 (July 1966), 76, 118. Un-
     der the title of "Fame" this was anthologized in I Don't
     Need You Any More. New York: Viking, 1967, pp.
     118-74; and The Portable AM, ed. Harold Clurman.
     New York: Viking, 1971, pp. 495-502 (The subtitle of
     "Recognitions" is "Once You Become Famous, Nobody
     Knows Who You Are").

36. "A Search for a Future," Saturday Evening Post, 239
     (August 13, 1966), 64-68; also The Best American Short
     Stories, 1967, ed. Martha Foley and David Burnett.
     Boston: Houghton Mifflin, 1967; and I Don't Need You
     Any More, pp. 224-40.

3. NON-FICTION (ARTICLES, ESSAYS, PUBLISHED LETTERS, AND REVIEWS)

37. "After the Fall: An Author's View," New Haven Register (April 25, 1965), Features, 9.

38. "The Age of Abdication [Anti-Vietnam War Criticism]," New York Times, December 23, 1967, p. 22: 3.

39. "An American Reaction," World Theatre, 1 (1951), 21-22 (reply to article in same issue by Walter Prichard Eaton, "Can the Gift of Playwriting Be Learned?").

40. "The American Theatre," Holiday, 17 (January 1955), 90-104; Also in The Pursuit of Learning, ed. Nathan Comfort Starr. New York: Harcourt, Brace, 1956; A Contemporary Reader, ed. Harry W. Rudman and Irving Rosenthal. New York: Ronald, 1961; AM, "Death of a Salesman": Text and Criticism, ed. Gerald Weales, pp. 151-55.

41. "AM Talks," Michigan Quarterly Review, 6 (Summer 1967), 153-84.

42. "AM vs. Lincoln Center," New York Times, April 16, 1972, II, 3 and 5.

43. "Art and Commitment," Anvil and Student Partisan, 11 (Winter 1960), 5.

44. Autobiographical Statement (Untitled), Twentieth Century Authors, First Supplement, ed. Stanley J. Kunitz. New York: Wilson, 1955, pp. 669-70.

45. "Banned in Russia," New York Times, December 10, 1970, pp. 47: 1.

46. "The Battle of Chicago: from the Delegates' Side," New York Times, September 15, 1968, VI, 29-31.

7

47. "Book in Hiding by Ronald Fraser; Reviewed by AM,"
     New York Times, July 9, 1972, VII, 1 (R).

48. "The Bored and the Violent," Harper's, 225 (November
     1962), 50-56. Also in First Person Singular, ed. Her-
     bert Gold. New York: Dial, 1963.

49. "A Boy Grew in Brooklyn," Holiday, 17 (March 1955),
     54-55, 117-24.

50. "Brewed in The Crucible," New York Times, March 9,
     1958, II, 3; AM, "The Crucible" : Text and Criticism,
     ed. Gerald Weales, pp. 169-73.

51. "Bridge to a Savage World," Esquire, 50 (October
     1958), 185-90.

52. "Broadway, from O'Neill to Now," New York Times,
     December 21, 1969, II, 1 & 7.

53. "Concerning the Boom," International Theatre Annual
     (No. 1), ed. Harold Hobson. London: John Calder,
     1956, pp. 85-88.

54. "Death of a Salesman," New York Times, February 27,
     1949, II, 1:5 (excerpts from Preface by AM).

55. "Death of a Salesman: AM Article on Play's First An-
     niversary," New York Times, February 5, 1950, II, 1:
     6.

56. "Death of a Salesman: A Symposium," Tulane Drama
     Review, 2 (May 1958), 63-9.

57. "The Family in Modern Drama," Atlantic, 197 (April
     1956), 35-41; also in Modern Drama, eds. Travis Bo-
     gard and William Oliver. New York: Oxford Univer-
     sity Press, 1965.

58. "Foreword, After the Fall," Saturday Evening Post,
     237 (February 1, 1964), 32.

59. "Global Dramatist: Author Views Reactions to His
     Plays Abroad," New York Times, July 21, 1952, II, 1
     (Death of a Salesman).

60. "Introduction" to AM's Collected Plays, pp. 3-55. New

York: Viking, 1957. Also in condensed form in _Play-wrights and Playwriting_. ed. by Toby Cole, New York: Hill & Wang, 1960; _AM_, "Death of a Salesman": _Text and Criticism_, ed. Gerald Weales, pp. 155-71; _AM_, "The Crucible" : _Text and Criticism_, ed. Gerald Weales, pp. 161-69.

61. "It Could Happen Here and It Did, [_The Crucible_ (CBS)]," _New York Times_, April 30, 1967, II, 17:3.

62. "Journey to _The Crucible_: Visit to Salem Recalled," _New York Times_, January 19, 1964, II, 1 & 3.

63. "Kidnapped," _Saturday Evening Post_, 242 (January 25, 1969), 40-42, 78-82.

64. "Limited Hang-Out," _Harper's_, 249 (September 1974), 13-14, 16, 20.

65. "Lincoln Repertory Theatre--Challenge and Hope," _New York Times_, January 19, 1964, II, 1 & 3.

66. "Literature and Mass Communications," _World Theatre_, 15 (Autumn 1966), 164-67.

67. "Mailbag on Adaptation," _New York Times_, November 29, 1959, II, 13 (Letter).

68. "Making Crowds," _Esquire_, 78 (November 1972), 160-61.

69. "Many Writers: Few Plays," _New York Times_, August 10, 1952, II, 1; _AM_, "The Crucible": _Text and Criticism_, ed. Gerald Weales. New York: Viking, 1971, pp. 157-61.

70. "The Measure of Things Is Man," _The American Theatre, 1970-71_, by International Theatre Institute. New York: Scribner's, 1972, pp. 96-97.

71. "Men and Words in Prison," _New York Times_, October 16, 1971, p. 31: 2.

72. "M's Article," _New York Times_, February 8, 1953, II, 3:1 (_The Crucible_).

73. "M's Comments on Filming of One-Act Play; Illus,"

New York Times, Nov. 17, 1969, p. 58:1 (The Reason Why).

74. "M's Comment on National Theatre, London, Staged by Sir L. Olivier ... The Crucible," New York Times, January 24, 1965, p. 82: 3.

75. "Miracles," Esquire, 80 (September 1973), 112-15.

76. "A Modest Proposal for the Pacification of Public Temper," Nation, 179 (3 July, 1954), 5-8.

77. "My Wife Marilyn," Life, 45 (December 22, 1958), 146-47.

78. "The Nature of Tragedy," New York Herald Tribune, March 27, 1949, V, 1-2.

79. "A New Era in American Theatre?" Drama Survey, 3 (1963), 70-71.

80. "On Recognition," Michigan Quarterly Review, 2 (Autumn 1963), 213-20.

81. "On Social Plays," Preface to A View from the Bridge. New York: Viking, 1955, pp. 1-18. Reprinted as "A View of One-Actors," New York Times, Sept. 25, 1955, II, 1, 3; also in Two Modern American Tragedies, ed. John D. Hurrell. New York: Scribner's, 1961.

82. "Our Guilt for the World's Evil," New York Times Magazine, January 3, 1965, pp. 10-11, 48 (Incident at Vichy).

83. "Our True Identity," New York Times Magazine, April 13, 1975, p. 111.

84. "Picking a Cast," New York Times, August 21, 1955, II, 1.

85. "The Playwright and the Atomic World," Colorado Quarterly, 5 (1956), 117-37; also in Tulane Drama Review, 5 (June 1961), 3-20; Theatre in the Twentieth Century, ed. Robert W. Corrigan. New York: Grove, 1963.

86. "Politics as Theater [Commenting on President Nixon's appeal to and Senator McGovern's lack of appeal to Americans]," New York Times, November 4, 1972, p. 33:2.

87. "Preface," An Enemy of the People. New York: Viking, 1951, pp. 7-12.

88. "Preface to A View from the Bridge" (Two-Act Version). New York: Compass, 1960, pp. v-x.

89. "Preface to The Crucible," Twentieth Century Drama: England, Ireland, the United States, ed. Ruby Cohen and Bernard F. Dukore. New York: Random House, 1966, pp. 535-40.

90. "A Review of Books in Hiding: The Life of Manuel Cortes by Ronald Fraser," New York Times, July 9, 1972, VII, 1 (R).

91. "The Role of P.E.N.," Saturday Review, 99 (June 4, 1966), 16-26.

92. "The Salesman Has a Birthday," New York Times, February 5, 1950, II, 1 (Death of a Salesman).

93. "The Shadows of the Gods: A Critical View of the American Theatre," Harper's 217 (August 1958), 35-43.

94. Short Reply (untitled) to an Article in the same issue by John Gassner, "Modern Drama and Society." World Theatre, 4 (Autumn, 1955), 40-41.

95. "Subsidized Theatre," New York Times, June 22, 1947, II, 1.

96. "Topics: On the Shooting of Robert Kennedy," New York Times, June 8, 1968, p. 30.

97. "Tragedy and Common Man," New York Times, February 27, 1949, II, 1 & 3; also in Theatre Arts, 35 (March 1951), 35, 48-50; AM, "Death of a Salesman": Text and Criticism, ed. Gerald Weales. New York: Viking, 1967, pp. 147-50.

98. "The University of Michigan," Holiday, 14 (December 1953), 41, 68-71, 128-32; 136-37, 140-43; also in

Points of Departure, ed. A. J. Carr and W. R. Stein-hoff. New York: Harper's, 1960, pp. 199-214.

99. Untitled Comment, World Theatre, 4 (Autumn 1955), 40-41.

100. "Viewing A View from the Bridge," Theatre Arts, 40 (September 1956), 31-32 (excerpt from the Preface).

101. "What Makes Plays Endure?" New York Times, August 15, 1965, II, 1 & 3.

102. "What's Wrong with This Picture?" Esquire, 82 (July 1974), 124-25, 170.

103. "When Life Had at Least Form," New York Times, January 24, 1971, II, 17:4.

104. "With Respect for Her Agony ... But with Love," Life, 56 (February 7, 1964), 66 (After the Fall).

105. "The Writer in America," Mainstream, (July, 1957), 43-46 (speech delivered in May 1957).

106. "Writers in Prison," Encounter, 30 (June 1968), 60-1.

107. "The Writer's Position in America," Coastlines, 2 (Autumn 1957), 38-40.

4. REPORTAGE

108. <u>In Russia</u> (with Inge Morath).   New York: Viking, 1969.
    "In Russia: Excerpts," <u>Harper's</u> 239 (September 1969), 37-78.

109. <u>Situation Normal.</u>   New York: Reynal and Hitchcock, 1944.
    "Their First Look at Live Bullets," <u>Science Digest</u>, 17 (April, 1945), 73-76 (excerpt in condensed form).

5. POEMS

110. "Lines from California: Poem," <u>Harper's</u> 238 (May 1969), 97; <u>The Portable AM</u>, ed. Harold Clurman. New York: Viking, 1971, pp. 561-62.

PART II:

SECONDARY SOURCES

(PUBLISHED AND UNPUBLISHED

WORKS ABOUT ARTHUR MILLER)

1. BOOKS AND BOOKLETS

111. Bloom, Lynne G. "The Crucible": A Critical Commentary. New York: R.D.M. Corp., 1964.

112. Calandra, Denis M. "The Crucible" Notes. Lincoln, Nebraska: Cliffs, 1968.

113. Corrigan, Robert W., ed. AM: A Collection of Critical Essays. Englewood Cliffs, N.J.: Prentice-Hall, 1969.
   Contents: Robert W. Corrigan, "Introduction: The Achievement of AM," pp. 1-22. Eric Mottram, "AM: The Development of a Political Dramatist in America," pp. 23-57 [American Theatre (Stratford-upon-Avon Studies, No. 10), ed. by John Russell Brown and Bernard Harris. London: Edward Arnolds, 1967]. Tom F. Driver, "Strength and Weakness in AM," pp. 59-67 [Tulane Drama Review, 4 (1960), 45-52]. Raymond Williams, "The Realism of AM," pp. 69-79 [Critical Q., 1 (Summer 1959), 140-49]. M. W. Steinberg, "AM and the Idea of Modern Tragedy," pp. 81-93 [Dalhousie Review, 40 (1960), 329-40]. Brian Parker, "Point of View in AM's Death of a Salesman," pp. 95-109 [Preface to AM's Collected Plays (New York: Viking, 1960); Tulane Drama Review, 2 (1958); "Tragedy and the Common Man," Theatre Arts, 35 (1951), 48-50]. Robert Warsaw, "The Liberal Conscience in The Crucible," pp. 111-21 [The Immediate Experience by Robert Warsaw (New York: Doubleday, 1962)]. Herbert Blau, "The Whole Man and the Real Witch," pp. 123-30 [The Impossible Theatre (New York: Macmillan, 1964)]. Gerald Weale's, "AM's Shifting Image of Man," pp. 131-42 [The American Theatre Today ed. Alan S. Downer (New York: Basic Books, 1967)]. Harold Clurman, "AM's Later Plays," pp. 143-68 ["AM: Theme and Variations," Theatre I (New York: Hill and Wang, 1964); "Director's

Notes: Incident at Vichy," TDR, 9 (1965), 77-90;
"The Merits of Mr. M.," New York Times, April
21, 1968, II, 1 and 3]. Chronology, pp. 169-70;
Selected Bibliography, pp. 173-76.

114. Esslinger, Pat. Barron's Simplified Approach to AM.
Woodburg, N.Y.: Barron's Educational Series, 1972.

115. Evans, Richard I. Psychology and AM. New York:
Dutton, 1969.
Contents: The Writer as Creator; The Writer and
Psychology; The Writer and Society.

116. Ferres, J. H., ed. Twentieth Century Interpretation
of "The Crucible." Englewood-Cliffs, N.J.: Prentice-
Hall, 1972.

117. Hayashi, Tetsumaro. AM Criticism (1930-1967). Metuchen, N.J.: Scarecrow, 1969.

118. Hayman, Ronald. AM. New York: Ungar, 1970 (1972)
[London: Heinemann, 1970].
Contents: Chronology, pp. 1-2; Interview with AM,
pp. 3-21; All My Sons, pp. 22-36; Death of a Salesman, pp. 37-56; The Crucible, pp. 57-69; A Memory of Two Mondays, pp. 70-75; A View from the
Bridge, pp. 76-83; After the Fall, pp. 84-95; Incident at Vichy, pp. 96-100; The Price, pp. 101-10;
Conclusion, pp. 111-22; Stage Production, pp. 123-
25; Cast List of Original Productions, pp. 126-31;
Bibliography, pp. 132-34.

119. Hogan, Robert Goode. AM [Pamphlets on American
Writers, No. 40]. Minneapolis: Univ. of Minnesota
Press, 1964.

120. Hubbard, E. D. and Truelson, Patricia. Death of a
Salesman: A Critical Commentary. New York: American R.D.M., 1967.

121. Huftel, Sheila. AM: The Burning Glass. New York:
Citadel, 1965; London: Wilt Allen, 1965.
Contents: Introduction. Author's Note. Acknowl-
edgements. 1. AM, 2. Focus, 3. M on Play-
writing, 4. The Man Who Had All the Luck, 5.
All My Sons, 6. Death of a Salesman, 7. The
Crucible, 8. A View from the Bridge, 9. The

Misfits, 10. After the Fall, 11. Incident at Vichy. Casts. Index.

122. Huttar, Charles. AM. New York: Everyman's Library, 1967; New Haven: College and University Press, 1968.

123. Meserve, Walter J. The Merrill Studies in "Death of a Salesman." Columbus, Ohio: Merrill, 1972.

124. Monarch Series. Review Notes and Study Guide to M's "The Crucible," "A View from the Bridge." New York: Monarch, 1965.

125. Moss, Leonard. AM (U.S. Author Series). New York: Twayne, 1967. New Haven, Conn.: College and University Press, 1968.
Contents: 1. The Man, 2, The Early Work, 3. Death of a Salesman, 4. Four "Social Plays," 5. After the Fall and Incident at Vichy. 6. The Perspective of a Playwright. Notes and References. Selected Bibliography. Index.

126. Murray, Edward. AM, Dramatist. New York: Ungar, 1967.
Contents: Preface, pp. vii-viii; All My Sons, pp. 1-21; Death of a Salesman, pp. 22-51; The Crucible, pp. 52-75; A Memory of Two Mondays, pp. 76-94; A View from the Bridge, pp. 95-124; After the Fall, pp. 125-57; Incident at Vichy, pp. 158-78; Conclusion, pp. 179-82. Bibliography.

127. Nelson, Benjamin. AM: Portrait of a Playwright. New York: McKay, 1970; London: Peter Owen, 1970.
Contents: Introduction. 1. "It'll be all out of mind as soon as you turn the corner"; 2. "I fell in love with the place"; 3. "A preview of coming attractions"; 4. "Of pussycats and plumbers"; 5. "Far from being a waste and a failure"; 6. "It doesn't matter anyway. Does it?"; 7. "An adjustment of distance to make a clear image"; 8. "To him they were all my sons, and I guess they were"; 9. "The play grew from simple images"; 10. "I am not a dime a dozen!"; 11. "To demonstrate that Ibsen is really pertinent today"; 12. "Because it is my name!"; 13. "My objection is, he refuses to repent"; 14. "I'll come back sometime. I'll visit

you"; 15. "And yet it is better to settle for half,
it must be!"; 16. "Everything's always changing,
isn't it?"; 17. "We are very dangerous!"; 18.
"They stand there, forever incomprehensible to one
another"; 19. "I just didn't want him to end up on
the grass"; 20. "Only connect." Selected Bibliography. Index.

128. Nourse, Joan Thelluson. AM's "Death of a Salesman"
and "All My Sons." New York: Monarch Press, 1965.

129. _____. AM's "The Crucible," "A Memory of Two
Mondays," "A View from the Bridge," "After the Fall,"
"Incident at Vichy." New York: Monarch Press, 1965.

130. _____. Monarch Literature Notes on M's "The Crucible" and "A View from the Bridge." New York:
Monarch Press, 1973.

131. Partridge, C. J. The Crucible. Oxford: Blackwell,
1971.

132. _____. Death of a Salesman. Oxford: Blackwell,
1969.

133. Roberts, James L. "Death of a Salesman": Notes.
Lincoln, Nebraska: Cliff's Notes, 1964.

134. Weales, Gerald, ed. AM, "The Crucible": Text and
Criticism. New York: Viking Press, 1967 (1971).
Contents: The Crucible: The Text : Criticism and
Analogues by AM / The Crucible in Production:
Comments & Reviews.

135. Welland, Dennis. AM. New York: Grove, 1961. Ed-
inburgh, Scotland: Oliver and Boyd, 1961. Magnolia,
Mass.: Peter Smith, 1961.
Contents: 1. The Facts, 2. The Fiction, 3. Be-
ginnings in Realism, 4. Death of a Salesman, 5.
The Devil in Salem, 6. Two New York Plays, 7.
The Drama, the Family, and Society. New York
Productions of Miller's Plays. Bibliography.

136. White, Sidney Howard. Guide to AM. (Merrill Guides.)
Columbus, Ohio: Charles E. Merrill, 1970.

2. ESSAYS IN BOOKS

137. Adamczewski, Zygmunt. "The Tragic Loss--Loman the Salesman," The Tragic Protest. The Hague: Nizhoff, 1963, pp. 172-92 (Death of a Salesman).

138. Allen, Walter C. "Inge Morath (photograph) and AM's In Russia," Library Journal Book Review. New York: Bowker, 1970, p. 316 (R).

139. Archer, William. "All My Sons," Play-Making. New York: Dover, 1960, passim.

140. Atkinson, Brooks. "All My Sons," Broadway Scrapbook. New York: Theatre Arts, 1947, pp. 277-79.

141. _____. "Death of a Salesman," Foreword to New Voices in the American Theatre. New York: Modern Library, 1955, pp. viii-ix.

142. Aughtry, Charles Edward, ed. "AM," Landmarks in Modern Drama from Ibsen to Ionesco. Boston: Houghton, Mifflin, 1963, pp. 596-97, passim.

143. Aylen, Leo. "AM," Greek Tragedy and the Modern World. London: Methuen, 1964, pp. 248-57.

144. Bader, A. L., ed. "On Recognition," To the Young Writer. Ann Arbor: University of Michigan Press, 1965, pp. 166-80.

145. Bentley, Eric. "The American Drama, 1944-1954," The Theatre of Commitment, and Other Essays on Drama in Our Society. New York: Atheneum, 1967, pp. 18-46.

146. _____. In Search of Theatre. New York: Knopf, 1953; London: Dobson, 1954, pp. 31-32, 80-84, 85-86, passim (Death of a Salesman).

21

147. _____. "Innocence of AM," Dramatic Event. New
York: Horizon Press, 1954, pp. 90-94 (The Crucible).

148. _____. "The Innocence of AM," What Is Theatre?
New York: Atheneum, 1968, pp. 62-65; AM, "The Crucible": Text and Criticism, ed. Gerald Weales, pp.
204-09.

149. _____, ed. The Play: A Critical Anthology. Engle-
wood Cliffs, N. J.: Prentice-Hall, 1962, pp. 729-49
(Death of a Salesman).
Contents: Atkinson, Brooks. "At the Theatre,"
New York Times, Feb. 11, 1949, p. 27 ... in pp.
729-31. Brown, Ivor. New York Times Maga-
zine, August 28, 1949 ... in pp. 732-36. Brown,
John Mason. "Seeing Things," Saturday Review of
Literature, Feb. 26, 1946 ... in pp. 736-41.
Clark, Eleanor. Partisan Review, 16 (June 1949),
631-36 ... in pp. 741-46. Morgan, Frederic K.
"Notes on the Theatre," Hudson Review, 2 (Sum-
mer 1949), 50-51 ... in pp. 746-47.

150. _____. The Playwright as Thinker. New York:
Harcourt Brace, 1955, passim (Incident at Vichy).

151. Bergler, Edmund. The Basic Neurosis. New York:
Grune & Stratton, 1949, passim (A View from the
Bridge).

152. Berkerman, Bernard and Siegman, Howard, eds. On
Stage: Selected Theatre Reviews from the "New York
Times," 1920-1970. New York: Arno Press Book/New
York Times, 1973, pp. 275, 298, 344, and 456.

153. Bierman, Judah, et al., eds. The Dramatic Experience. Englewood Cliffs, N. J.: Prentice-Hall, 1958,
pp. 490-93; AM, "Death of a Salesman" : Text and
Criticism, ed. Gerald Weales, pp. 265-71, passim.

154. Bigsby, C. W. E. "AM," Confrontation and Commitment: A Study of Contemporary American Drama,
1959-1966. London: MacGibbon & Kee, 1968; Columbia: University of Missouri Press, 1968, pp. 26-49.

155. Blau, Herbert. "Counterforce I: The Social Drama,"
The Impossible Theatre. New York: Macmillan, 1964.
[n. p.]; AM, "The Crucible": Text and Criticism, ed.

Gerald Weales, pp. 231-38.

156. Bone, Larry Earl. "AM's I Don't Need You Any
     More," Library Journal Book Review. New York:
     Bowker, 1968, p. 674 (R).

157. Brossard, Chandler, ed. "The Crucible," Scene Before
     You: a New Approach to American Culture. New
     York: Rinehart, 1955, pp. 191-203.

158. Broussard, Louis. American Drama: Contemporary
     Allegory from Eugene O'Neill to Tennessee Williams.
     Norman: University of Oklahoma Pr., 1963, pp. 117,
     120 (The Crucible, Death of a Salesman, The Man Who
     Had All the Luck, & A View from the Bridge).

159. Brown, John Mason. Dramatis Personae: A Retro-
     spective Show. New York: Viking, 1951, pp. 16, 29-
     30, 94-100, 535; AM, "Death of a Salesman": Text
     and Criticism, ed. Gerald Weales. New York: Viking,
     1967, pp. 205-11.

160. _____. Still Seeing Things. New York: McGraw-
     Hill, 1950, pp. 196-204 (All My Sons and Death of a
     Salesman).

161. Brustein, R. S. "AM's Mea Culpa," Seasons of Dis-
     content, by R. S. Brustein, New York: Simon & Schu-
     ster, 1965, pp. 243-47 (After the Fall).

162. _____. "Muddy Track at Lincoln Center," Seasons
     of Discontent. New York: Simon and Schuster, 1965,
     pp. 259-63.

163. _____. "The Unseriousness of AM," The Third The-
     atre. New York: Knopf, 1969, pp. 103-06.

164. Buck, Richard M. "The Creation of the World and Oth-
     er Business," Library Journal Book Review, 1973.
     New York: Bowker, 1973, p. 609 (R).

165. Cassidy, Carl. "Claudia Cassidy Reviews Death of a
     Salesman," Passionate Playgoer, ed. G. Oppenheimer.
     New York: Viking, 1958, pp. 600-01.

166. Clurman, Harold. "Death of a Salesman," Lies Like
     Truth: Theatre Reviews and Essays. New York:

Macmillan, 1958, pp. 68-72; Also in Two Modern
American Tragedies, ed. John D. Hurrell. New York:
Scribner's, 1961, pp. 65-67 (R); AM, "Death of a
Salesman": Text and Criticism, ed. Gerald Weales,
pp. 212-16.

167. Cohn, Ruby. "The Articulate Victims of AM," Dia-
logue in American Drama. Bloomington: Indiana University Press, 1971, pp. 68-96 (O'Neill, AM, T. Williams, Albee).

168. Cole, Toby, ed. Playwrights on Playwriting; the Mean-
ing and Making of Modern Drama from Ibsen to Ionesco.
New York: Hill & Wang, 1960, pp. 261-76 (Death of a
Salesman).

169. Corrigan, Robert W. "The Achievement of AM," The
Theatre in Search of a Fix. New York: Delacorte
Press, 1973, pp. 325-47.

170. Dekle, Bernard. Profiles of Modern American Authors.
Rutland, Vt.: Tuttle, 1969, pp. 147-53.

171. Downer, Alan S. Fifty Years of American Drama,
1900-1950. Chicago: Regnery, 1951, pp. 52-53, 73-
75 (All My Sons and Death of a Salesman).

172. _____. Recent American Drama. Minneapolis:
Univ. of Minn. Press, 1961, passim (The Crucible).
(pamphlet)

173. Dunning, Stephen and Sams, Henry W., eds. Scholarly
Appraisals of Literary Works Taught in High Schools.
Champaign, Ill.: National Council of Teachers of Eng-
lish, 1965, pp. 110-17 (The Crucible).

174. Dusenbury, Winifred L. "Personal Failure," The
Theme of Loneliness in Modern American Drama.
Gainesville: Univ. of Florida Press, 1960, pp. 8-37
(Death of a Salesman).

175. Ethridge, James E. and Kopaler, Barbara, eds. Contemporary Authors. Detroit: Gale Research Co., 1962
(1967), pp. 665-66.

176. Fergusson. Francis. The Idea of a Theater. Princeton, N.J.: Princeton Univ. Press, 1949, passim

(After the Fall).

177. Foster, Richard J. "Confusion and Tragedy: The
Failure of M's Salesman." Two Modern American
Tragedies, ed. John D. Hurrell. New York: Scrib-
ner's, 1961, pp. 82-88.

178. Freedman, Morris. American Drama in Social Con-
text. Carbondale: Southern Illinois Univ. Press, 1971,
passim (chapters on O'Neill, T. S. Eliot, AM).

179. _____. "Bertolt Brecht and American Social Dra-
mas," The Moral Impulse. Carbondale: Southern Illinois Press, 1967, pp. 99-114.

180. Frenz, H., ed. "Tragedy and the Common Man,"
American Playwrights on Drama. New York: Hill &
Wang, 1965, pp. 134-53.

181. Gardner, Rufus Hallette. The Splintered Stage. New
York: Macmillan, 1965, passim.

182. Gascoigne, Bamber. "AM," Twentieth-Century Drama,
London: Hutchinson University, 1962, pp. 174-83.

183. Gassner, John. "Affirmation? M's The Crucible, As
Event and Play," Theatre at the Crossroad. New York:
Rinehart, 1960, pp. 274-78.

184. _____. "Death of a Salesman: First Impression,
1949," Theatre in Our Times. New York: Crown,
1954, pp. 364-73; AM, "Death of a Salesman": Text
and Criticism, ed. Gerald Weales, pp. 231-39.

185. _____. Form and Idea in Modern Theatre. New
York: Dryden, 1956, pp. 109-49, passim (Death of a
Salesman).

186. _____. "The Lincoln Center Repertory Company:
After the Fall," Dramatic Soundings. New York:
Crown Publishers, 1968, pp. 547-50.

187. _____. "The Lincoln Center Repertory Company:
Incident at Vichy," Dramatic Soundings. New York:
Crown Publishers, 1968, pp. 550-52.

188. _____. "New American Playwrights: Williams, M,

and Others," in <u>On Contemporary Literature</u>, ed. Richard Kostelanetz. New York: Avon Books, 1964, pp. 48-63.

189.   _____. "New American Playwrights: Williams, M, and Others," <u>The Theatre in Our Time.</u> New York: Crown, 1954, pp. 364-73.

190.   _____. <u>Theatre at the Crossroads.</u> New York and London: Holt, Rinehart & Winston, 1960, <u>passim</u> (Death of a Salesman).

191.   _____. <u>The Theatre in Our Times.</u> New York: Crown, 1954, pp. 342-55, <u>passim</u> (Death of a Salesman).

192.   _____. and Allen, R. G., eds. "A Note on the Historical Accuracy of <u>The Crucible</u>; excerpt from <u>The Crucible</u>," <u>Theatre and Drama in the Making.</u> Boston: Houghton Mifflin, 1964, pp. 848-57.

193.   Geisinger, Marion. "AM," <u>Plays, Players, & Playwrights.</u> New York: Hart Pub. Co., 1971, pp. 590-650, <u>passim.</u>

194.   Gilman, R. "Getting It Off His Chest, But Is It Art?" <u>Common and Uncommon Masks.</u> New York: Random House, 1971, pp. 156-59.

195.   _____. "Still Falling," <u>Common and Uncommon Masks.</u> New York: Random House, 1971, pp. 152-55.

196.   Gold, Herbert, ed. "The Bored and the Violent," <u>First Person Singular.</u> New York: Dial, 1963, pp. 173-84.

197.   Goode, James. <u>The Story of the Misfits.</u> Indianapolis: Bobbs-Merrill, 1963, <u>passim.</u>

198.   Gordon, Lois. "<u>Death of a Salesman</u>: An Appreciation," <u>The Forties,</u> ed. by Warren French, Deland, Fla.: Everett/Edwards, 1969, pp. 273-83.

199.   Gould, Jean R. "AM," <u>Modern American Playwrights.</u> New York: Dodd, Mead, 1966, pp. 247-63.

200.   Grigson, Geoffrey, ed. <u>The Concise Encyclopedia of Modern World Literature.</u> New York: Hawthorn Books,

1963, pp. 244-45.

201. Gross, Theodore L., ed. Representative Men. New York: Free Press, 1970, pp. 276-77.

202. Gruen, John. Close Up. New York: Viking, 1968, pp. 58-63.

203. Hagopian, John V. "Death of a Salesman," Insight, Frankfurt: Hirschgraben, 1962, I, 174-86.

204. Harte, Barbara and Riley, Carolyn. 200 Contemporary Authors. Detroit: Gale, 1969, pp. 189-91.

205. Hayman, Ronald. Playback. New York: Horizon, 1974, pp. 111-26.

206. Heilman, Robert B. "AM," The Iceman, the Arsonist, and the Troubled Agent. Seattle: University of Washington Press, 1969, pp. 142-61.

207. Hewitt, Barnard. Theatre U.S.A. 1668 to 1957. New York: McGraw-Hill, 1959, pp. 444-48, 471 (All My Sons and Death of a Salesman).

208. Hogan, Robert Goode, and Molin, Sven Eric, eds. Drama: The Major Genres: An Introductory Critical Anthology. New York: Dodd, Mead, 1963, pp. 5, 195, 265, 633; "On Social Plays," pp. 20-21.

209. Huftel, Sheila. AM: The Burning Glass. New York: Citadel, 1965, pp. 146-47; "More on Danforth," AM, "The Crucible": Text and Criticism, ed. Gerald Weales, pp. 173-74.

210. Hughes, Catherine R. "The Crucible," Plays, Politics, and Polemics. New York: Drama Book Specialist Pub., 1973, pp. 15-25.

211. Hughes, Glenn. A History of the American Theatre 1700-1950. New York: Samuel French, 1951, pp. 461, 467-68, 473-74, 479 (All My Sons & Death of a Salesman.)

212. Hurrell, John D. Two Modern American Tragedies: Review and Criticisms of "Death of a Salesman" and "A Streetcar Named Desire." New York: Scribner,

1961, pp. 54-88 (reprinted criticism).

213. Jung, Carl Gustav. The Undiscovered Self. New York: New American Library, 1957, passim (After the Fall).

214. Kaufmann, Walter. From Shakespeare to Existentialism: Studies in Poetry, Religion, and Philosophy. Boston: Beacon Press, 1959, pp. 27, 332.

215. Kazan, Elia. "Excerpts from Kazan's Notebooks for Death of a Salesman (Untitled)," A Theater in Your Head, ed. Kenneth Thorpe Rowe. New York: Funk & Wagnalls, 1960, pp. 44-59.

216. Kerr, Walter. "Albee, M, Williams: The View from the Mirror," Thirty Plays Hath November. New York: Simon & Schuster, 1969, pp. 214-20.

217. _____. How Not to Write a Play. New York: Simon & Schuster, 1955, passim (The Crucible).

218. Kitchin, Lawrence. Mid-Century Drama. London: Faber & Faber, 1960, pp. 57-64 (Death of a Salesman).

219. Krutch, Joseph Wood. The American Drama Since 1918: An Informal History. New York: Braziller, 1957, pp. 324-25, 328-29 (Death of a Salesman).

220. _____. "Modernism" in Modern Drama. Ithaca, N.Y.: Cornell University Press, 1953, pp. 102, 106, 123-30.

221. Kunitz, Stanley Jasspon, ed. Twentieth Century Authors: 1st Supplement. New York: Wilson, 1955, pp. 669-70.

222. Leaska, Mitchell A. "M," The Voice of Tragedy. New York: Speller, 1963, pp. 273-78 (Death of a Salesman).

223. Lerner, Max. "Ethics of the Dust," Actions and Passions. New York: Simon & Schuster, 1949, pp. 20-28 (All My Sons).

224. Lewis, Allan. "The American Scene--Tennessee Williams and AM," The Contemporary Theatre. New York: Crown, 1962, pp. 282-303 (Death of a Salesman).

225. _____. "AM--Return to the Self," American Plays
     and Playwrights of the Contemporary Theatre. New
     York: Crown Publishers, 1965, pp. 35-52 (After the
     Fall).

226. _____. The Contemporary Theatre. New York:
     Crown, 1962, pp. 282-302.

227. Lumley, F. "Broadway Cortege--Tennessee Williams
     and AM," New Trends in 20th Century Drama. New
     York: Oxford Univ. Press, 1960; London: Barrie &
     Rockcliff, 1960, pp. 182-99, passim.

228. McCarthy, Mary. Sights and Spectacles 1937-1956.
     New York: Farrar, Straus and Cudahy, 1956, pp.
     xxiv-xxvi.

229. McCollum, William G. Tragedy. New York: Farrar,
     Straus & Cudahy, 1957; London: Heinemann, 1959, pp.
     16-17 (Death of a Salesman).

230. Madden, David, ed. American Dream, American Night-
     mares. Carbondale: Southern Illinois University Press,
     1970, passim.

231. Magill, Frank Northen, ed. Cyclopedia of World Au-
     thors. New York: Harper, 1958, pp. 754-55.

232. Mander, John. "AM's Death of a Salesman," The
     Writer and Commitment. Philadelphia: Dufour, 1962,
     pp. 138-52.

233. Mielziner, Jo. "Designing a Play: Death of a Sales-
     man," Designing for the Theatre. New York: Athen-
     eum, 1965, [n. p.]; AM, "Death of a Salesman": Text
     and Criticism, ed. Gerald Weales. New York: Viking
     1967, pp. 187-98.

234. "M. , A. ," American People's Encyclopedia, 12 (1965),
     472.

235. "M. , A. ," Chambers's Encyclopedia, 9 (1971), 405.

236. "M. , A. ," Collier's Encyclopedia, 16 (1971), 259.

237. "M. , A. ," Current Biography, 8 (Oct. 1947), 39-40;
     34 (Feb. 1973), 296-98.

238. "M., A.," Encyclopaedia Britannica, 15 (1970), 465.

239. "M., A.," Encyclopedia Americana, 19 (1970), 117.

240. "M., A.," Encyclopedia International, 12 (1964), 94.

241. "M., A.," Encyclopedia Judaica, 11 (1971), 1579.

242. "M., A.," The International Who's Who, 1965-66.
     London: Europa, 1965, p. 774.

243. "M., A.," New Caxton Encyclopedia, 13 (1970), 4058.

244. "M., A.," "A Note on the Historical Accuracy of The
     Crucible. Excerpts from The Crucible," Theatre and
     Drama in the Making, eds. J. Gassner & R. G. Allen,
     pp. 848-57.

245. "M., A.," Twentieth Century Authors, ed. Stanley J.
     Kunitz and Vineta Colby. New York: Wilson, 1955, pp.
     669-70 (1st Supplement).

246. "M., A.," Who's Who in America. Vol. 33. Chi-
     cago: Marquis Who's Who, 1972, p. 2183.

247. "M., A.," Who's Who in the Theatre, ed. John Parker.
     Bath, England: Pitman Pub., 1972, pp. 1180-87.

248. "M., A.," World Book Encyclopedia, 13 (1971), 468.

249. Miller, Jordan Y. American Dramatic Literature: Ten
     Modern Plays in Historical Perspective. New York:
     McGraw-Hill, 1961, pp. 558-59.

250. "M's Influence upon Swedish Drama," The International
     Year Book, 1949. New York: Funk & Wagnalls, 1950,
     p. 537.

251. Moody, Walter D. "The Know-It-All Salesman," Men
     Who Sell Things. Chicago: McClurg, 1909; AM, "Death
     of a Salesman": Text and Criticism, ed. Gerald
     Weales, pp. 367-70.

252. Morehouse, Ward. Matinee Tomorrow. New York:
     Whittlesey House, 1949, pp. 291-92 (All My Sons).

253. Morris, Lloyd. Curtain Time: The Story of the Amer-

ican Theater. New York: Random House, 1953, p.
362.

254. Muller, Herbert J. The Spirit of Tragedy. New York:
Knopf, 1956, pp. 316-17 (Death of a Salesman).

255. Murray, Edward. "AM--Death of a Salesman, The
Misfits and After the Fall," The Cinematic Imagination.
New York: Ungar, 1972, pp. 69-85 (film adaptations).

256. Nannes, Casper H. Politics and the American Drama.
Washington, D.C.: The Catholic University of American Press, 1960, pp. 184-85 (The Crucible).

257. Nathan, George Jean. "American Playwrights, Old and
New: "AM," Theatre in the Fifties, 1953, pp. 105-09
(The Crucible).

258. _____. "Death of a Salesman," Theatre Book of the
Year, 1948-1949. New York: Knopf, 1949, pp. 279-
85; Also in Two Modern American Tragedies, ed. John
D. Hurrell, pp. 57-60 (R).

259. _____. "An Enemy of the People," Theatre Book of
the Year, 1950-1951. New York: Knopf, 1951, pp.
167-70.

260. _____. The Magic Mirror. New York: Knopf,
1960, pp. 243-50 (Death of a Salesman). Also in The
Theatre Book of the Year, 1948-1949.

261. _____. "Man Who Had All the Luck," Theatre Book
of the Year, 1944-1945, pp. 171-73.

262. _____. The Theatre Book of the Year, 1946-1947.
New York: Knopf, 1947, pp. 290-93 (All My Sons).

263. _____. The Theatre of the Fifties. New York:
Knopf, 1953, pp. 105-09.

264. _____, ed. "All My Sons," Theatre Book of the
Year, 1946-1947. New York: Knopf, 1948, pp. 290-93.

265. The New International Year Book, 1965. New York:
Funk & Wagnalls, 1966, p. 467 (Incident at Vichy).

266. New York Theatre Critics' Reviews. New York:

Critics' Theatre Reviews, Inc., 1947, pp. 358, 73,
475-78 (All My Sons, Death of a Salesman, The Man
Who Had All the Luck).

267. Nyren, Dorothy, ed. A Library of Literary Criticism:
Modern American Literature. New York: Ungar, 1960,
pp. 337-41.
Contents:
1. Young, Stark. "All My Sons," New Republic,
116 (February 10, 1947), 42.
2. Phelan, Kappo. "All My Sons," Commonweal,
45 (February 14, 1947), 445-46.
3. Clurman, Harold. "Death of a Salesman," New
Republic 118 (February 28, 1949), 27.
4. Gabriel, Gilbert W. "Death of a Salesman,"
Theatre Arts, 23 (April 1949), 15.
5. Gassner, John. "Death of a Salesman," Forum, 111 (April 1949), 219-22.
6. Wyatt, Euphemia Van Rensselaer. "Death of
a Salesman," Catholic World 169 (April 1949),
62-63.
7. Shea, Albert A. "Death of a Salesman," Canadian Forum, 29 (July 1949), 86-89.
8. Schneider, Daniel E. "Death of a Salesman,"
Theatre Arts, 33 (October 1949), 18-20.
9. Hayes, Richard. "The Crucible," Commonweal, 57 (February 20, 1953), 498.
10. Kirchwey, Freda. "The Crucible," Nation,
175 (February 7, 1953), 131-32.
11. Hewes, Henry. "AM," Saturday Review, 36
(October 15, 1955), 25-26.
12. Rovere, Richard H. "AM," New Republic,
(June 17, 1957), 13.

268. Olson, Elder. Tragedy and the Theory of Drama. Detroit: Wayne State Univ. Press, 1961, passim (The
Crucible and Death of a Salesman).

269. Oppenheimer, George, ed. Passionate Playgoer; a Personal Scrapbook. New York: Viking, 1958, pp. 600-
601 (Death of a Salesman).

270. Popkin, Henry. "AM: The Strange Encounter," American Drama and Its Critics, ed. Alan Seymour Downer.
Chicago: Univ. of Chicago Press, 1965, pp. 218-39.

271. _____, and Weales, Gerald. "All My Sons, The

Crucible and Death of a Salesman," A Time of Harvest, ed. Robert E. Spiller. New York: Hill & Wang, 1964, pp. 123-36, 142.

272. Porter, T. E. "Acres of Diamonds: Death of a Salesman," Myth and Modern American Drama. Detroit: Wayne State Univ. Press, 1969, pp. 127-52.

273. _____. "The Long Shadow of the Law: The Crucible," Myth and Modern American Drama. Detroit: Wayne State Univ. Press, 1969, pp. 177-99.

274. Rahv, Phillip. "AM and the Fallacy of Profundity," Literature and the Sixth Sense. Boston: Houghton Mifflin, 1970, pp. 385-91.

275. _____. "AM and the Fallacy of Profundity," The Myth and the Power House. New York: Farrar, Straus & Giroux, 1965, pp. 225-33 (Incident at Vichy).

276. Raines, Mary Bozeman. "AM's The Price," Library Journal Book Review. New York: Bowker, 1968, p. 656 (R).

277. Rama, Murphy, V. American Expressionistic Drama (containing analyses of three outstanding American plays: O'Neill, The Hairy Ape; Tennessee Williams, The Glass Menagerie; AM, Death of a Salesman). Delhi: Doaba House, 1970, passim.

278. Raphael, D.D. The Paradox of Tragedy. London: G. Allen & Unwin, 1960, pp. 103-05 (The Crucible).

279. The Reader's Encyclopedia of American Literature, ed. Max J. Herzberg and the Staff of the Thomas Y. Crowell Co. New York: Crowell, 1962, pp. 737-38.

280. Riley, Carolyn, ed. Contemporary Literary Criticism. Detroit: Gale Research Co., 1973, pp. 215-19.

281. _____, and Harte, Barbara, eds. Contemporary Literary Criticism. Detroit: Gale Research, 1974, pp. 278-90.

282. Rovere, Richard H. "The Conscience of AM," The American Establishment, and Other Reports, Opinions, and Speculations. New York: Harcourt, Brace &

World, 1962, pp. 276-84.

283. Schneider, Daniel E. "A Study of Two Plays by AM,"
     The Psychoanalyst and the Artist. New York: Interna-
     tional Univ. Press, 1950, pp. 241-56 (All My Sons and
     Death of a Salesman); also in AM, "Death of a Sales-
     man": Text and Criticism, ed. Gerald Weales, pp.
     250-58.

284. Sharpe, Robert Boies. Irony in the Drama. Chapel
     Hill: Univ. of North Carolina Press, 1959, pp. 194-
     95, 195-97, passim.

285. Sheed, W. "A View from the Bridge," The Morning
     After. New York: Farrar, Straus & Giroux, 1971,
     pp. 168-71.

286. Sievers, W. David. Freud on Broadway: A History of
     Psychoanalysis and the American Drama. New York:
     Hermitage House, 1955, pp. 376-80, passim.

287. _____. "Tennessee Williams and AM," Freud on
     Broadway: A History of Psychoanalysis and the Amer-
     ican Drama. New York: Hermitage House, 1955, pp.
     376-80, 388, 391-96; also in Two Modern American
     Tragedies, ed. John D. Hurrell, pp. 139-45.

288. Stambusky, Alan A. "AM: Aristotelian Canons in the
     20th Century Drama," Modern American Drama, ed.
     William E. Taylor. Deland, Fla.: Everett/Edwards,
     1968.

289. Steinbeck, John. "The Trial of AM," Contemporary
     Moral Issues, ed. Harry K. Girvetz. Belmont, Calif.:
     Wadsworth, 1963, pp. 72-74.

290. Tynan, Kenneth. "American Blues: the Plays of AM
     and Tennessee Williams, Excerpts from Curtains," The
     Modern American Theatre, ed. Alvin B. Kernan.
     Englewood Cliffs, N.J.: Prentice-Hall, 1967, pp. 34-
     44.

291. _____. "The Crucible by AM at the Bristol Old
     Vic," Curtains; Selections from the Drama Criticism
     and Related Writings. New York: Atheneum, 1961,
     pp. 253-54.

292. _____. Curtains. New York: Atheneum, 1961, pp.
253-54, 257-62, passim.

293. Vinson, James, ed. Author and Dramatist. New York:
St. Martin's, 1973, pp. 540-44.

294. Wager, Walter, ed. The Playwrights Speak. New
York: Dell Pub. Co., 1967, pp. 1-24.

295. Warfel, Harry Redcay. American Novelists of Today.
New York: American Book Co., 1951, pp. 301-02.

296. Warshow, Robert. "The Liberal Conscience in The
Crucible," The Immediate Experience: Movies, Comics,
Theatre and Other Aspects of Popular Culture. Garden
City, N.Y.: Doubleday, 1962, pp. 189-203; AM, "The
Crucible": Text and Criticism, ed. Gerald Weales,
pp. 210-26.

297. Watts, Richard, Jr. "Introduction," The Crucible.
New York: Bantam, 1959, pp. ix-xiv.

298. Weales, Gerald C. "AM," The American Theatre Today, ed. A. S. Downer. New York: Basic Books,
1967, pp. 85-98.

299. _____. "AM: Man and His Image," American Dra-
ma Since World War II. New York: Harcourt, Brace
& World 1960, pp. 3 17; AM, "Death of a Salesman":
Text and Criticism, ed. Gerald Weales, pp. 350-66;
AM, "The Crucible": Text and Criticism, ed. Gerald
Weales, pp. 333-51.

300. _____. "Williams and M.," The Jumping Off Place.
New York: Macmillan, 1969, pp. 1-23.

301. Welty, Eudora. A Curtain of Green and Other Stories.
New York: Harcourt, Brace & World, 1941; AM,
"Death of a Salesman": Text and Criticism, ed. Ger-
ald Weales, pp. 371-85.

302. Whitman, Robert F. The Play Reader's Handbook.
Indianapolis: Bobbs-Merrill, 1966, pp. 61-62 (The
Crucible).

303. _____. The Play Reader's Handbook. Indianapolis:
Bobbs-Merrill, 1966, pp. 31-32, 46-49 (Death of a
Salesman).

304. Williams, R. "From Hero to Victim: the Making of
     Liberal Tragedy, to Ibsen and M," Modern Tragedy.
     Stanford, Calif.: Stanford Univ. Press, 1966; London:
     Chatto & Windus, 1966, pp. 87-105.

305. Zolotow, Maurice. Marilyn Monroe. New York: Ban-
     tam, 1961; London: W. H. Allen, 1961, pp. 260-70,
     passim.

3. DOCTORAL DISSERTATIONS

306. Ashley, Franklin Bascom. "The Theme of Guilt and Responsibility in the Plays of AM," University of South Carolina, 1970 [DAI, 31(1971), 5349A].

307. Bettenbausen, Elizabeth A. "Forgiving the Idiot in the House: Existential Anxiety in Plays by AM and Its Implications for Christian Ethics," University of Iowa, 1972 [DAI, 32A (1972), 7076A].

308. Blades, Larry Thomas. "Williams, M. and Albee: A Comparative Study," St. Louis University, 1971 [DAI, 32A (1972), 4600A].

309. Epstein, Arthur D. "AM's Major Plays: A Critical Study," Indiana University, 1969 [DAI, 30 (1970), 4983A].

310. Fisher, William J. "Trends in Post-Depression American Drama: A Study of the Works of William Saroyan, Tennessee Williams, Irwin Shaw, and AM," New York University, 1952 [No DA entry].

311. Flanagan, James K. "AM: A Study in Sources and Themes," University of Notre Dame, 1969 [DAI, 30 (1970), 4984A].

312. Fleming, William P. "Tragedy in American Drama: The Tragic Views of Eugene O'Neill, Tennessee Williams, AM, and Edward Albee," University of Toledo, 1972 [DAI, 33A (1972), 308A].

313. Geier, Woodrow A. "Images of Man in Five American Dramatists: A Theological Critique," Vanderbilt University, 1959 [DA, 20 (1959), p. 1463-64].

314. Harrow, Kenneth J. "The Transformation of the Rebel: A Comparative Study of the Works and Development of

Albert Camus, AM, and Ignazio Silone," New York University, 1970 [DAI, 31 (1971), 6609A-10A].

315. Jacobson, Irving Frederic. "The Fallen Family: A Study in the Works of AM," University of California, Los Angeles, 1974 [DAI, 35A (1974), 2271A-72A].

316. Johnson, Robert Garrett. "A General Semantic Analysis of Three of AM's Plays: Death of a Salesman, The Crucible, and All My Sons," University of Denver, 1963 [DA, 24 (1964), p. 5610].

317. Johnson, Vernon Elso. "Dramatic Influences in the Development of AM's Concept of Social Tragedy," George Peabody College for Teachers, 1962 [DA, 23 (1962), pp. 2135-36].

318. Lavi, Gay Heit. "Children of Civilization Fall Together: A Study of Style and Language in the Plays of AM," University of Pittsburgh, 1971 [DAI, 32 (1971), 1518A].

319. Leopold, Vivian Ruth. "Man and Society in the Plays of AM," New York University, 1971 [DA, 32 (1971), 2833A].

320. Long, Madeleine J. "Sartrean Themes in Contemporary American Literature," Columbia University, 1967 [DA, 28 (1967), 1439A].

321. McMahon, Helen Marie. "AM's Common Man: The Problem of the Realistic and the Mythic," Purdue University, 1972 [DAI, 34A (1973), 326A].

322. Manske, Dwain E. "A Study of the Changing Family Roles in the Early Published and Unpublished Works of AM, to Which Is Appended a Catalogue of the AM Collection at the University of Texas at Austin," University of Texas, 1970 [DAI, 32 (1972), 4008A].

323. Martin, Robert Allen. "The Major Plays and Critical Thought of AM to the Collected Plays," University of Michigan, 1965 [DA, 26 (1965), 2755-56].

324. Murray, Edward James. "Structure, Character, and Theme in the Plays of AM," University of Southern California, 1966 [DA, 27 (1966), 1061A-62A].

325. Scanlan, Thomas M. "The American Family and Family Dilemmas in American Drama," University of Minnesota, 1970 [DAI, 32 (1971), 1529A]. (Esp. O'Neill, AM, T. Williams.)

326. Sheldon, Neil. "Social Commentary in the Plays of Clifford Odets and AM," New York University, 1963 [DA, 24 (1964), 3018-19].

327. Slavensky, Sonia W. "Suicide in the Plays of AM, A View from Glory Mountain," Loyola University of Chicago, 1973 [DAI, 33A (1973), 1936A].

328. Stephens, Suzanne Schaddelee. "The Dual Influence: A Dramaturgical Study of the Plays of Edward Albee and the Specific Dramatic Forms and Themes Which Influenced Them," Miami University, 1972 [DAI, 34A (1973), 342A].

329. Van Allen, Harold. "An Examination of the Reception and Critical Evaluation of the Plays of AM in West Germany from 1950-1961," University of Arkansas, 1964 [DA, 25 (1964), p. 1901].

330. Welch, Charles A. "Guilt in Selected Plays of AM: A Phenomenological Inquiry and Creative Response," United States International University, 1972 [DAI, 33A (1972), 1031A].

331. West, Constance Catherine. "The Use of Persuasion in Selected Plays of AM," University of Minnesota, 1968 [DA, 29 (1969), p. 3718A].

332. Zurcher, Carl Donald. "An Analysis of Selected American Criticism of the Plays of AM in the Light of His Own Commentary of Drama," Purdue University, 1973 [DAI, 35A (1974), 619A-20A].

4. MASTER'S THESES

333. Aaron, Chloe W. "AM: Evolution of an American Playwright," George Washington University, 1966.

334. Barden, Mary L. "A Critical Analysis of Moral Concepts in Three Plays of AM," University of Houston, 1962.

335. Barrett, Elizabeth T. "The Role of Law in AM's Drama," University of Alberta (Canada), 1966.

336. Bradley, Carol A. "AM's Use of Ibsen's Retrospective Exposition," Ohio State University, 1969.

337. Burge, Barbara J. "AM: Social Critic," University of Pittsburgh, 1961.

338. Caldwell, Michael S. "AM: A Critical Analysis of Candida," Henderson State College, [n. d.].

339. Campbell, Dorothy. "AM: A Critical Analysis of the Play All My Sons," Henderson State College, [n. d.].

340. Chapman, George. "Death of a Salesman: A Psychological Study," Texas Arts and Industries University, 1950.

341. Clark, J. W. "AM's Death of a Salesman: An Instance of Modern Tragedy," Wesleyan University, 1958.

342. Constable, C. R. "All My Sons by AM," Ohio State University, 1949.

343. DeWaide, Sandia L. "The Female Characters in the Plays of AM," San Diego State College, 1967.

344. Ellison, Jerome. "God on Broadway." South Connecticut State College, 1966 [A. M. et al].

40

345. Erwin, Martin N. "The Use of Blocks of Past Time in AM's Death of a Salesman," University of North Carolina at Chapel Hill, 1965.

346. Fisher, William C. "Death of a Salesman: A Drama for the High School Performer," Texas Christian University, 1969.

347. Flannery, Cathleen B. "The Theme of Responsibility in the Plays of AM," University of Maryland at College Park, 1966.

348. Fleming, Isabelle R. "Chekhovian Influence & Parallels in the Works of T. Williams and AM," Columbia University, 1954.

349. Foreman, Howard E. "AM and Modern Tragedy," Colorado State University, 1967.

350. Freling, Roger N. "A Study of the Principal Characters in AM's Plays," Oklahoma State University, 1961.

351. Funk, Elaine M. "The Crucible as Drama and Polemic," University of Maryland at College Park, 1968.

352. Gentry, Glenda E. "Spatial Form in AM's Death of a Salesman and After the Fall," University of Redlands, 1965.

353. Gilliard, Frederick W. "Dignity in AM's Drama," University of Montana, 1965.

354. Goodsell, G. D. "Tragic Elements in the Major Plays of AM," University of Utah, 1953.

355. Hannett, Beverly A. "A Twentieth Century Morality Play: AM's Death of a Salesman," State University of New York at Buffalo, 1966.

356. Heemann, Paul W. "AM's The Crucible: A Study of the Playwright's Dramatic Theory and Method," University of North Carolina at Chapel Hill, 1959.

357. Heiss, Rolland L. "The Search for Identity and Love in AM's Plays," Ball State University, 1969.

358. Hitchens, Gordon. "Attention Must Be Paid: A Study

of Social Values in Four Plays by AM," Columbia University, 1962.

359. Hoy, J. C. "Contemporary American Society as Reflected in the Plays of AM," Wesleyan University, 1960.

360. Inserillo, Charles R. "Wish and Desire: Two Poles of the Imagination in the Drama of AM and T. S. Eliot," Xavier University of Louisiana, 1962.

361. McAnany, Emile G. "The Tragic Commitment: A Study of AM's Heroes in His Plays and His Critical Writings," St. Louis University, 1960.

362. McBride, Jane M. "An Existential Examination of AM," University of Houston, 1963.

363. Mittelstet, Sharron R. "Social Conscience in AM," West Texas State University, 1968.

364. Moor, Gulliume. "Form and Meaning in AM's After the Fall," Roosevelt University at Chicago, 1966.

365. Moss, Leonard. "The Tragic Theme in Two American Playwrights, Maxwell Anderson and AM," Indiana University, 1954.

366. Polhemus, Ann S. "AM and Greek Tragedy," University of North Carolina at Chapel Hill, 1960.

367. Priddy, Barbara H. "The Fall of the Fortress: Thematic Progression in AM's Major Plays," University of Louisville, 1969.

368. Reyer, Paul. "AM's Concept of Tragedy: Its Application to His Works," University of Arkansas, 1952.

369. Ringer, Linda K. "Human Relationships in the Major Works of AM," Baylor University, 1965.

370. Schwalb, Sanford. "Thematic Developments in AM's Plays," University of Tennessee, 1965.

371. Show, Gregory. "Three Views of the Puritans: Whittier, M, and O'Neill," Wayne State University, 1965.

372. Smith, Phyllis S. "AM: A Writer of Tragedy," East

Carolina University, 1967.

373. Spiller, Ellen B. "The Influence of Henrik Ibsen on AM," University of Houston, 1965.

374. Stanley, Linda C. "Guilt in AM," University of Rhode Island, 1966.

375. Stark, Howard J. "AM's Concept of Tragedy," University of the Pacific, 1962.

376. Swan, Mary B. "Attitude Towards the American Dream in Selected Plays of Edward Albee and AM," University of Rhode Island, 1965.

377. Swett, T. W. "An Appraisal of AM's Concept of Tragedy," University of Southern California, 1953.

378. Towle, Calvin K. "A Study of Puritanism as Seen by Nathaniel Hawthorne in The Scarlet Letter and by AM in The Crucible," Columbia University, 1961.

379. Wilkinson, Richard T. "AM Manuscripts at the University of Texas," University of Texas, 1964.

380. Wood, Carolann. "AM: Is It Possible for the Individual to Shape His Own Destiny?" University of Massachusetts, 1967.

381. Worth, Deane. "An Examination of AM's Death of a Salesman in the Light of Aristotle's Idea of Action, Plot and the Tragic Hero," Smith College, 1950.

382. Young, Miriam. "The Decline of the Tragic Figure in American Literature as Seen in Historical Perspective: A Study of Captain Ahab and Willy Loman as Opposite Figures in the Decline," Columbia University, 1964 (Death of a Salesman).

5. INTERVIEWS, DIALOGS, AND SYMPOSIA
   WITH ARTHUR MILLER

383. Allsop, Kenneth. "A Conversation with AM," Encounter,
     13 (July 1959), 58-60.

384. "AM Talks," Michigan Quarterly Review, 6 (Summer
     1967), 153-84.

385. "The Art of the Theatre II," Paris Review, 10 (Sum-
     mer 1966), 61-98.

386. Barthel, Joan. "AM Ponders The Price," New York
     Times. January 28, 1968, II, 1 and 5.

387. Brandon, Henry. "Conversation with AM," World The-
     atre, 11 (Autumn 1962), 229-40; London Sunday Times,
     March 20, 1960; also in Harper's, 221 (November 1960),
     63-69.

388. _____. "The State of the Theatre: A Conversation
     with AM," London Sunday Times, March 20, 1960; also
     in Harper's, 221 (November 1960), 63-69; As We Are,
     ed. Henry Brandon. New York: Doubleday, 1961;
     World Theatre, 11 (1962), 229-40.

389. Carlisle, Olga, and Styron, Rose. "The Art of the
     Theatre II: AM, an Interview," Paris Review, 10 (Sum-
     mer 1966), 61-98.

390. "Death of a Salesman: A Symposium," Tulane Drama
     Review, 2 (May 1958), 63-69.

391. "Death of a Salesman: M Discusses Writing the Play,"
     New York Times, February 6, 1949, II, 1:5.

392. Evans, Richard Isadore. Psychology & AM (Dialogues).
     New York: Dutton, 1969.

393. Fallaci, O.   "Apropos of After the Fall." World
      Theatre, 14 (January 1965), 79+.

394. Feron, James.   "M in London to See The Crucible,"
      New York Times, January 24, 1965, p. 82.

395. Gelb, Barbara.   "Question: 'Am I My Brother's Keep-
      er?' " New York Times, November 29, 1964, II, 1 &
      3.

396. Gelb, Phillip.   "Morality and Modern Drama," Educa-
      tional Theatre Journal, 10 (October 1958), 190-202;
      AM, "Death of a Salesman": Text and Criticism, ed.
      Gerald Weales. New York: Viking, 1967, pp. 172-86.

397. _____.   "A Symposium with AM, Gore Vidal, Rich-
      ard Watts, John Beaufort, Martin Dworkin, David W.
      Thompson, and Phillip Gelb as Moderator," Tulane Dra-
      ma Review, 2 (May 1958), 63-69; Two Modern Ameri-
      can Tragedies, ed. John D. Hurrell. New York:
      Scribner's, 1961, pp. 76-81 (Death of a Salesman).

398. Goyen, William.   "AM's Quest for Truth," New York
      Herald Tribune Magazine, January 19, 1964, p. 35.

399. Greenfield, Joseph.   " 'Writing Plays Is Absolutely
      Senseless,' AM Says, 'But I Love It. I Just Love It,' "
      New York Times, February 13, 1972, VI, 16. [See
      also entry 1158.]

400. Griffin, John & Alice.   "AM Discusses The Crucible;
      Interview," Theater Arts, 37 (October 1953), 33-34, 67.

401. Gruen, Joseph.   "Portrait of the Playwright at Fifty,"
      New York Times, October 24, 1965, pp. 12-13.

402. No entry.

403. Harris, J.   "M and Director J. Harris Interview on
      Subject Matter," New York Times, February 8, 1953,
      p. 30:1 (The Crucible).

404. Hayman, Ronald.   "Interview with AM," AM. New
      York: Ungar, 1972, pp. 3-21.

405. Herbert, Edward T., ed.   "Eugene O'Neill: An Evalu-

tion by Fellow Playwrights," <u>Modern Drama,</u> 6 (1963), 239-40.

406. Hewes, Henry. "Broadway Postscript: AM and How He Went to the Devil," <u>Saturday Review,</u> 36 (January 1953), 24-26.

407. _____, ed. "American Playwrights Self-Appraised" (Short Answers to a Questionnaire), <u>Saturday Review,</u> 38 (September 3, 1955), 18-19 (Interview).

408. Huston, John. "Conversation at St. Cleraus Between AM and John Huston," <u>Manchester Guardian,</u> November 3, 1960. p. 8 (<u>The Misfits</u>).

409. Hyams, Barry. "A Theatre: Heart and Mind," <u>Theatre: Annual of the Repertory Theater of Lincoln Center,</u> 1 (1964), 56-61.

410. "<u>Incident at Vichy</u>: M Charges Soviet Press Twisted Review of Play into Propaganda; an Interview in Moscow," <u>New York Times,</u> February 3, 1965, p. 30:4.

411. "Literature and Mass Communications," <u>World Theatre,</u> 15 (1966), 164-67 (excerpts from a talk given to the Pen Club Congress in Bled, Yugoslavia).

412. McClean, L. "American Weekend; A View from the Country with AM," <u>Vogue,</u> 159 (March 15, 1972), 102-09 (Interview).

413. Martin, Robert A. "AM and Meaning of Tragedy," <u>Modern Drama,</u> 13 (1970), 34-39.

414. _____. "AM--Tragedy and Commitment," <u>Michigan Quarterly Review,</u> 8 (1969), 176-78 (Interview).

415. _____. "The Creative Experience of AM: An Interview," <u>Educational Theater Journal,</u> 21 (October 1969), 310-17.

416. Morley, Sheridan. "M on M," <u>Theatre World,</u> 61 (March 1965), 4, 8.

417. "New Insurgency: Excerpts from Address, May 19, 1968," <u>Nation,</u> 206 (July 3, 1968), 717.

418. "Notes and Comment; Concerning Article in the Times," New Yorker, 43 (January 13, 1968), 19.

419. "On Recognition," Michigan Quarterly Review, 2 (1963), 213-20 (Speech).

420. "P.E.N. Politics and Literature: Summary of Address," Publisher's Weekly, 190 (July 18, 1966), 32-3.

421. "The Plaster Masks," Encore, 9 (April 1946), 50.

422. Samachson, Dorothy and Joseph. Let's Meet the Theatre. New York: Abelard-Schuman, 1954, pp. 15-20.

423. Schumach, Murray. "AM Grew Up in Brooklyn," New York Times, February 6, 1949, II, 1 & 3.

424. "Search for a Future," Saturday Evening Post, 239 (August 13, 1966), 64-68.

425. Shanley, John P. "M's 'Focus' on TV Today," New York Times, January 21, 1962, II, 19.

426. Stevens, Virginia. "Seven Young Broadway Artists," Theatre Arts, 31 (June 1947), 56 (All My Sons).

427. "Their First Look at Live Bullets," Science Digest, 17 (April 1945), 73-76.

428. U.S. House of Representatives, Committee on Un-American Activities. Investigation of the Unauthorized Use of United States Passports, Part 4, June 21, 1956. Washington: U.S. Government Printing Office, November, 1956. ("Interview" is not exactly the best word for this item.)

429. Wallace, Mike. "AM Talks with Mike Wallace and Arnold Gingrich: The Contemporary Theatre and Freedom in Mass Media," Michigan Quarterly Review, 6 (Summer, 1967), 153-84.

430. Wolfert, Ira. "AM, Playwright In Search of His Identity," New York Herald Tribune, January 25, 1953, IV, 3.

431. "The Writer's Position in America," Coastlines, 8 (Autumn 1957), 38-40.

6. PERIODICAL ARTICLES AND REVIEWS

432. Adler, Henry. "To Hell with Society," Tulane Drama Review, 4 (May, 1960), 53-76; also in Theatre in the Twentieth Century, ed. Robert W. Corrigan. New York: Grove Press, 1963.

433. "After the Fall," Life, 56 (February 7, 1964), 64 (R).

434. "After the Fall," New York Review of Books, 2 (March 5, 1964), 4 (R).

435. "After the Fall," Prairie Schooner, 39 (Spring 1965), 92 (R).

436. "After the Fall," Time, 83 (January 31, 1964), 54 (R).

437. "After the Fall," Virginia Quarterly Review, 40 (Summer 1964), cxii (R).

438. "After the Fall: AM's Return," Newsweek, 63 (February 3, 1964), 49-52.

439. "All My Sons," Booklist, 43 (March 15, 1947), 220 (R).

440. "All My Sons," Life, 22 (March 10, 1947), 71-72, 74.

441. "All My Sons," Newsweek, 29 (February 10, 1947), 85 (R).

442. "All My Sons," Time, 46 (February 10, 1947), 68, 70; 49 (February 10, 1947), 68 (R).

443. "All My Sons," Time, 51 (April 12, 1948), 100 + (FR).

444. "All My Sons Criticism," New Yorker, 50 (November 11, 1974), 106-07.

445. "All My Sons: Father and Sons," Newsweek, 31 (April

12, 1948), 89 (FR).

446. "All My Sons: Talented Young Dramatist Unites the
Season's First Serious Hit about War's Aftermath,"
Life, 22 (March 10, 1947), 71-72.

447. Alpert, Hollis. "The Misfits," Saturday Review, 44
(February 4, 1961), 27, 47 (FR).

448. _____. "Mr. M's Indignant Theme: Death of a
Salesman," Saturday Review of Literature, 34 (December 22, 1951), 34 (FR).

449. Angell, Roger. "The Current Cinema: Misfire," New
Yorker, 36 (February 4, 1961), 86, 88 (The Misfits).

450. _____. "The Misfits," New Yorker, 36 (February
4, 1961), 86 + (FR).

451. "AM: Act II," Economist, 183 (June 1, 1957), 790.

452. "AM Cleared of Contempt of Congress," Publishers'
Weekly, 174 (August 18, 1958), 26, 28.

453. "AM's Startling Play ... Is It Good Taste? Marilyn's
Ghost Takes the Stage," Life, 56 (February 7, 1964),
64A (After the Fall).

454. Atkinson, Brooks. "I Don't Need You Any More,"
Newsweek, 69 (February 27, 1967), 92 (R).

455. _____. "I Don't Need You Any More," Saturday Review, 50 (February 25, 1971), 53 (R).

456. _____, et al. New York Theatre Critics' Reviews,
5 (1944), 73-74 (The Man Who Had All the Luck); 8
(1947), 475-78 (All My Sons); 11 (1950), 154-56 (An
Enemy of the People); 14 (1953), 383-86 (The Crucible);
16 (1955), 272-75 (A View from the Bridge); 25 (1964),
374-78 (After the Fall).

457. _____, et al. New York Theatre Critics' Reviews,
10 (1949), 358-61 (Death of a Salesman).

458. Aymé, Marcel. "I Want to Be Hanged Like a Witch,"
tr. Gerald Weales, Arts, (December 15-21, 1954), 1 &
3; AM, "The Crucible": Text and Criticism, ed. Ger-

ald Weales, pp. 239-41.

459. Banerjee, Chinmoy. "AM: The Prospect of Tragedy,"
     English Miscellany (St. Stephen's College, Delhi), 3
     (1965), 66-76.

460. Barksdale, Richard K. "Social Background in the Plays
     of M and Williams," CLA Journal, 6 (March 1963), 161-
     69 (A View from the Bridge).

461. Barnett, Gene A. "The Theatre of Robert Bolt," Dal-
     housie Review, 48 (Spring 1968), 13-23 (Death of a
     Salesman).

462. Basseches, Maurice. "Situation Normal," Saturday Re-
     view of Literature, 27 (December 2, 1944), 64-66 (R).

463. Bates, Barclay W. "The Lost Past in Death of a
     Salesman," Modern Drama, 11 (September 1968), 164-
     72.

464. Baxandall, Lee. "AM: Still the Innocent," Encore, 11
     (May-June 1964), 16-19 (R); AM, "The Crucible": Text
     and Criticism, ed. Gerald Weales, pp. 352-58.

465. _____. "AM's Latest," Encore, 7 (March-April
     1965) 19-23 (Incident at Vichy).

466. Bellow, Saul. "Focus," Library Journal, 70 (October
     1945), 979 (R).

467. _____. "Focus," New Republic, 114 (January 7,
     1946), 29 (R).

468. Bentley, Eric. "Crush-ible: Do We Believe in Discus-
     sion?" New Republic, 135 (July 2, 1956), 2, 22 (The
     Crucible).

469. _____. "Death of a Salesman," Theatre Arts, 33
     (November 1949), 12-14 (R).

470. _____. "M's Innocence," New Republic, 128 (Febru-
     ary 16, 1953), 22-23 (The Crucible).

471. _____. "The Theater," New Republic, 133 (Decem-
     ber 19, 1955), 21-22 (Death of a Salesman and A View
     from the Bridge).

472. Bergeron, David M. "AM's The Crucible and Nathaniel Hawthorne: Some Parallels." English Journal, 58 (January 1969) 47-55.

473. Bergman, Herbert. "The Interior of a Heart: The Crucible and The Scarlet Letter," Univ. College Quarterly (Michigan State), 15 (1970), 27-32.

474. Berksdale, Richard K. "Social Background in the Plays of M and Williams," College Language Association Journal, 6 (March 1963), 161-69.

475. Berndtson, Arthur. "Tragedy as Power: Beyond Nietzsche," Bucknell Review, 15 (December 1967), 97-107.

476. Bettina, Sister M. "Willy Loman's Brother Ben: Tragic Insight in Death of a Salesman," Modern Drama, 4 (February 1962), 409-12.

477. Beyer, William H. "The State of the Theatre: Midseason Highlights," School and Society, 65 (April 5, 1947), 250-51 (All My Sons).

478. _____. "The State of the Theatre: Revivals 'Front and Center,'" School and Society, 73 (February 17, 1951), 105 (An Enemy of the People).

479. _____. "The State of the Theatre: The Devil at Large," School and Society, 77 (March 21, 1953), 185-86 (The Crucible).

480. _____. "The State of the Theatre: The Season Opens," School and Society, 70 (December 3, 1949), 363-64; AM: "Death of a Salesman": Text and Criticism, ed. Gerald Weales, pp. 228-30.

481. Bigsby, C. W. E. "The Fall and After: AM's Confession," Modern Drama, 10 (September 1967), 124-36 (After the Fall).

482. _____. "What Price AM?": An Analysis of The Price," Twentieth Century Literature, 16 (1970), 16-25.

483. Bleich, David. "Psychological Bases of Learning from Literature: AM's Death of a Salesman," College Eng-

lish, 33 (October 1971), 32-45.

484. Bliquez, Guerin. "Linda's Role in Death of a Salesman," Modern Drama, 10 (1968), 383-86.

485. Blocker, J. "PEN Pals," Newsweek, 66 (July 26, 1965), 92.

486. Blumberg, Paul. "Sociology and Social Literature: Work Alienation in the Plays of AM," American Quarterly, 21 (1969), [291]-310.

487. Bly, Robert. "The Dead World and the Live World," Sixties, 8 (Spring 1966), 2-7.

488. Boggs, W. Arthur. "Oedipus and All My Sons," Personalist, 42 (Autumn 1961), 555-60.

489. Boone, A. R. "How a Hollywood Cameraman Takes Home Movies," Popular Science, 139 (July 1941), 204-06.

490. Bottman, Philip N. "Quentin's Quest: AM's Move into Expressionism," Wisconsin Studies in Contemporary Literature, 5 (1968), 41-52.

491. Bradshear, William R. "The Empty Bench: Morality, Tragedy, and AM," Michigan Quarterly Review, 5 (1966), 270-78 (After the Fall).

492. Brahms, Caryl. "Marilyn, Dolly and Dylan," Spectator, 212 (February 14, 1964), 213 (After the Fall).

493. Brien, Alan. "There Was a Jolly M," Spectator, 201 (August 8, 1958), 191-92.

494. Bronson, David. "An Enemy of the People: A Key to AM's Art and Ethics," Comparative Drama, 2 (Winter 1968-69), 229-47.

495. Brown, John Mason. "The Crucible," Saturday Review, 36 (February 14, 1953), 41 (R).

496. _____. "New Talents and AM," Saturday Review of Literature, 30 (March 1, 1947), 22-24 (All My Sons).

497. _____. "Seeing Things: Even as You and I," Saturday Review of Literature, 32 (February 26, 1949),

30-32; also in The Play: A Critical Anthology, ed.
Eric Bentley, pp. 736-39 (Death of a Salesman).

498. _____. "Seeing Things: Witch-Hunting," Saturday
Review of Literature, 36 (February 14, 1953), 41-42
(The Crucible).

499. Brustein, Robert. "AM's Mea Culpa," New Republic,
150 (February 8, 1964), 26-28, 30 (After the Fall).

500. _____. "Muddy Track at Lincoln Center," New Republic, 151 (December 26, 1964), 26-27; also in his
Seasons of Discontent. New York: Simon & Schuster,
1965, pp. 259-63 (Incident at Vichy).

501. _____. "The Unseriousness of AM," New Republic,
158 (February 24, 1968), 38-41 (The Price).

502. _____. "Why American Plays Are Not Literature,"
Harper's, 219 (October 1959), 167-73.

503. Bryden, Ronald. "Dead Earnest," New Statesman, 71
(February 4, 1966), 170.

504. Buitenhuis, Peter. "AM: The Fall from the Bridge,"
Canadian Association for American Studies Bulletin, 3
(1967), 55-71.

505. Butterfield, Alfred. "Focus," New Republic, 114 (January 7, 1946), 29 (R).

506. Callahan, Elizabeth Amidon. "The Tragic Hero in Contemporary Secular & Religious Drama," Literary Half-
Yearly, 8 (January-July 1967), 42-49.

507. Caputi, Anthony. "The Shallows of Modern Serious Drama," Modern Drama, 4 (September 1961), 111-16.

508. Cassell, Richard A. "AM's 'Rage of Conscience,'"
Ball State Teachers College Forum, 1 (1960), 31-36 (All
My Sons).

509. Casty, Alan. "Post-Loverly Love: A Comparative Report," Antioch Review, 26 (Fall 1966), 399-411.

510. Charyn, Jerome. "A Review of I Don't Need You Any
More." Book World, (February 12, 1967), 4 (R).

511. "Cinema: New Picture," Time, 77 (February 3, 1961), 68 (The Misfits).

512. Clark, Eleanor. "Death of a Salesman," Partisan Review, 16 (1949), 631-35; reprinted in Two Modern American Tragedies, ed. by John D. Hurrell. New York: Scribner's, 1961, pp. 61-64.

513. _____. "Old Glamour, New Gloom," Partisan Review, 16 (June 1949), 631-36. Also in The Play: A Critical Anthology, ed. Eric Bentley. Englewood Cliffs, N. J.: Prentice-Hall, 1959, pp. 741-46; AM, "Death of a Salesman": Text and Criticism, ed. Gerald Weales. New York: Viking, 1967, pp. 217-23.

514. Clurman, Harold. "AM: Theme and Variations," Theatre (Lincoln Center), 1 (1964), 13-24.

515. _____. "The Crucible," Nation, 214 (May 15, 1972), 636-37 (R).

516. _____. "Death of a Salesman," Nation, 168 (March 5, 1949), 283 (R).

517. _____. "Director's Notes: Incident at Vichy," Tulane Drama Review, 9 (Summer 1965), 77-90.

518. _____. "An Enemy of the People," Nation, 212 (March 29, 1971), 411-13 (R).

519. _____. "The Price," Nation, 206 (February 26, 1968), 281-83 (R).

520. _____. "Theatre: Attention!" New Republic, 120 (February 28, 1949), 26-28 (Death of a Salesman) (R).

521. _____. "Theatre: Lear and Stockmann," New Republic, 124 (January 22, 1951), 21-22 (An Enemy of the People).

522. Coen, F. "Teaching the Drama; Ibsen's The Master Builder and M's All My Sons," English Journal, 56 (November 1967), 1136-39.

523. Coffey, Waven. "Tennessee Williams: The Playwright as Analysand," Ramparts, 1 (November 1962), 510-58.

524. Cogley, John. "Witnesses' Dilemma," Commonweal, 65 (March 15, 1957), 612.

525. Cohen, Marshall. "The Sin of the Sons," Atlantic, 221 (July 1968), 120-22 (The Price).

526. Cohen, Nathan. "Hollow Heart of a Hollow Drama," National Review, 16 (April 7, 1964), 289-90. (After the Fall).

527. "Collected Plays," Booklist, 53 (June 15, 1957), 523 (R).

528. Cook, Roderick. "I Don't Need You Any More," Harper's, 234 (March 1967), 136 (R).

529. Corrigan, Robert W. "The Achievements of AM," Comparative Drama, 2 (Fall 1968), 141-60.

530. Couchman, Gordon W. "AM's Tragedy of Babbitt," Educational Theatre Journal, 7 (October 1955), 206-11 (Death of a Salesman).

531. Covici, Pascal. "The Misfits," Southern Review, 46 (Spring 1961), ix-x (R).

532. Cowley, Malcolm. "Witches of Salem (The Crucible)," New Republic, 139 (December 22, 1958), 21 (FR).

533. "The Creation of the World and Other Business," New Republic, 167 (December 23, 1972), 26 + (R).

534. "The Crucible," American Record Guide, 29 (March 1963), 508-99 + (R).

535. "The Crucible," Booklist, 49 (May 15, 1953), 299 (R).

536. "The Crucible," Life, 34 (February 9, 1953), 87-88, 90 (R).

537. "The Crucible," New York Theatre Critics' Reviews, 1953, p. 383; 1964, p.295 (R).

538. "The Crucible," Newsweek, 41 (February 2, 1953), 68 (R).

539. "The Crucible," Time, 61 (February 2, 1953), 48 (R).

540. Curtis, Penelope. "The Crucible," Critical Review
     (formerly the Melborne Critical Review), 8 (1965), 45-
     48; AM, "The Crucible": Text and Criticism, ed. Ger-
     ald Weales, pp. 255-71.

541. Czimer, Jozsef. "Price and Value," New Hungarian
     Quarterly, 10, (Winter 1969), 169-76 (The Price).

542. De Schweinitz, George. "Death of a Salesman: A Note
     on Epic and Tragedy," Western Humanities Review, 14
     (Winter 1960), 91-96; AM, "Death of a Salesman":
     Text and Criticism, ed. Gerald Weales, pp. 272-79.

543. "Death of a Salesman," Booklist, 45 (May 1, 1949),
     289; 45 (May 15, 1949), 310 (R).

544. "Death of a Salesman," Christian Century, 69 (Febru-
     ary 20, 1952), 231 (FR).

545. "Death of a Salesman," Life, 26 (February 21, 1949),
     115 (R).

546. "Death of a Salesman," Life, 32 (January 14, 1952),
     63-64+ (FR).

547. "Death of a Salesman," Newsweek, 38 (December 31,
     1951), 56-57 (FR).

548. "Death of a Salesman," Time, 53 (February 21, 1949),
     74-76 (R).

549. "Death of a Salesman," Time, 58 (December 31, 1951),
     60 (FR).

550. Dedmon, Emmett. "Death of a Salesman," Catholic
     World, 169 (April 1949), 62 (R).

551. Deedy, J. "Creation of the World and Other Business,"
     Commonweal, 97 (January 5, 1973), 290 (R).

552. Dent, Allan. "The Misfits," Illustrated London News,
     238 (June 10, 1961), 992 (FR).

553. Dillingham, William B. "AM and the Loss of Con-
     sciousness," Emory University Quarterly, 16 (Spring
     1960), 40-50; AM, "Death of a Salesman": Text and
     Criticism, ed. Gerald Weales, pp. 339-49.

554. Donoghue, Denis. "The Human Image in Modern Drama," Lugano Review, 1 (1965), 155-68.

555. Douglas, James W. "M's The Crucible: Which Witch Is Which?" Renascence, 15 (Spring 1963), 145-51.

556. Downer, Alan S. "Mr. Williams and Mr. M," Furioso, 4 (1949), 66-70.

557. _____. "Old, New, Borrowed and (a Trifle) Blue: Notes on the New York Theatre, 1967-1968," Quarterly Journal of Speech, 54 (October 1968), 199-211.

558. Driver, Tom F. "AM's Pilgrimage," Reporter, 30 (February 27, 1964), 46-48 (After the Fall).

559. _____. "Strength and Weakness in AM," Tulane Drama Review, 4 (May 1960), 45-52 (Death of a Salesman).

560. Dudek, L. "AM and The Misfits," Delta, 15 (August 1961), 26-27.

561. Duprey, Richard A. "AM," Catholic World, 193 (September 1961), 394-95 (The Crucible and A View from the Bridge).

562. Durham, Frank. "A Review of Leonard Moss' Arthur Miller (New York: Twayne, 1967)," Southern Humanities Review, 2 (Winter 1968), 131-32 (R).

563. Eaton, W. P. "All My Sons," Library Journal, 72 (March 15, 1947), 466 (R).

564. _____. "Death of a Salesman," New Republic, 120 (February 28, 1949), 26 (R).

565. Edwards, John. "AM: An Appraisal," Time and Tide, 42 (May 4, 1961), 740-41 (The Misfits).

566. "End of a Famous Marriage with M. Monroe," Life, 49 (November 21, 1960), 88A-90.

567. "An Enemy of the People," Newsweek, 37 (January 8, 1951), 67 (R).

568. "An Enemy of the People," Time, 57 (January 8, 1951), 31.

569. "Engagement Party (M. Monroe)," Newsweek, 48 (July 2, 1956), 21-22.

570. Epstein, Arthur D. "A Look at A View from the Bridge," Univ. of Texas Studies in Literature and Languages, 7 (Spring 1965), 109-22.

571. Epstein, Leslie. "The Unhappiness of AM ... After the Fall, Incident at Vichy, and Lincoln Center," Tri-Quarterly, 1 (Spring 1965), 165-73.

572. Fender, Stephen. "Precision and Pseudo Precision in The Crucible," Journal of American Studies, 1 (April 1967), 87-98; AM, "The Crucible": Text and Criticism, ed. Gerald Weales, pp. 272-89.

573. Fergusson, Francis. "A Conversation with Digby R. Diehl," Transatlantic Review, 18 (Spring 1965), 115-21 (After the Fall).

574. Ferres, John H. "Still in the Present Tense: The Crucible Today," University College Quarterly, 17 (May 1972), 8-18.

575. Ferris, Oliver H.P. "An Echo of Milton in The Crucible," N & Q, 16 (1969), 268.

576. Field, B. S., Jr. "Hamartia in Death of a Salesman," Twentieth Century Literature, 18 (1972), 19-24.

577. Findlater, Richard. "No Time for Tragedy?" Twentieth Century, 161 (January 1957), 56-62 (A View from the Bridge).

578. Flaxman, Seymour L. "The Debt of Williams and M to Ibsen and Strindberg," Comparative Literature Studies, 1 (September 1963), 51-60.

579. Fleming, Peter. "The Theatre," Spectator, 180 (May 21, 1948), 612 (All My Sons).

580. _____. "The Theatre," Spectator, 183 (August 5, 1949), 173 (Death of a Salesman).

581. Forster, Peter. "The Misfits," Spectator, 206 (June 9, 1961), 840 (FR).

582. Freedley, George. "After the Fall," Library Journal, 89 (April 1, 1964), 1620 (R).

583. _____. "The Crucible," Library Journal, 78 (March 15, 1953), 920 (R).

584. _____. "Death of a Salesman," Library Journal, 74 (June 15, 1949), 74 (R).

585. _____. "Incident at Vichy," Library Journal, 90 (February 15, 1965), 892 (R).

586. _____. "The Misfits," Library Journal, 86 (March 15, 1961), 1155 (R).

587. _____. "A View from the Bridge," Library Journal, 81 (January 1, 1956), 101 (R).

588. French, Philip. "After the Fall," New Statesman, 74 (November 10, 1967), 651 (R).

589. Fruchter, Norm. "On the Frontier," Encore, 9 (January-February 1962), 17-27 (The Crucible and Death of a Salesman).

590. Fuller, A. Howard. "A Salesman Is Everybody," Fortune, 39 (May 1949), 79-80; AM, "Death of a Salesman"; Text and Criticism, ed. Gerald Weales, pp. 240-43.

591. Gabriel, Gilbert W. "Death of a Salesman," Theatre Arts, 33 (April 1949), 14-16. Excerpt in A Library of Literary Criticism, ed. Dorothy Nyren. New York: Ungar, 1960, p. 15 (Death of a Salesman).

592. Ganz, Arthur. "AM: After the Silence," Drama Survey, 3 (Fall 1964), 520-30 (After the Fall).

593. _____. "The Silence of AM," Drama Survey, 3 (October 1963), 335-47 (All My Sons, The Crucible, and Death of a Salesman).

594. Gargan, Edward T. "Reflections on Tunneling Out of an Ant Heap," [rev. of The Holocaust Kingdom], 81 Commonweal, 81 (February 12, 1965), 655 (Incident at Vichy) (R).

595. Garland, Robert. "Audience Spellbound by Prize Play
      of 1949 (Death of a Salesman)," New York Journal-
      American, February 11, 1949, p. 24; AM, "Death of
      a Salesman": Text and Criticism, ed. Gerald Weales.
      New York: Viking, 1967, pp. 199-201.

596. Gassner, John. "After the Fall," Educational Theatre
      Journal, 16 (May 1964), 177-79 (R).

597. _____. "Broadway in Review," Educational Theatre
      Journal, 16 (May 1964), 177-79 (After the Fall).

598. _____. "Modern Drama and Society," World The-
      atre, 4 (Autumn 1955), 34-35 (Reply by M, 40-41).

599. _____. "The Theatre Arts," Forum, 107 (March
      1947), 271-75 (All My Sons).

600. _____. "The Theatre Arts," Forum, 111 (April
      1949), 219-21; excerpt in A Library of Literary Criti-
      cism, ed. Dorothy Nyren. New York: Ungar, 1960,
      pp. 219-22 (Death of a Salesman).

601. _____. "Tragic Perspectives: A Sequence of Quer-
      ies," Tulane Drama Review, 2 (May 1958), 7-22
      (Death of a Salesman).

602. _____. "The Winter of Our Discontent," Theatre
      Arts, 39 (August 1955), 23-24, 86.

603. Gelb, Phillip. "Morality and Modern Drama," Educa-
      tional Theatre Journal, 10 (October 1958), 190-202.

604. Gentleman, David. "In Russia with Inge Morath," New
      Statesman, 78 (December 5, 1969), 824 (R).

605. Gianakaris, C. J. "Absurdism Altered: Rosencrantz
      and Guildenstern Are Dead," Drama Survey, 7 (Winter
      1968-69), 52-58.

606. Gibbs, Wolcott. "The Crucible," New Yorker, 28 (Jan.
      31, 1953), 47 (R).

607. _____. "Death of a Salesman," New Yorker, 24
      (February 19, 1949), 58-60 (R).

608. _____. "An Enemy of the People," New Yorker,

26 (January 13, 1951), 44 (R).

609. _____. "A Memory of Two Mondays," New Yorker,
31 (October 8, 1955), 92, 94-95 (R).

610. _____. "A View from the Bridge," New Yorker, 31
(October 8, 1955), 92, 94-95 (R).

611. Gilder, Rosamond. "All My Sons," Theatre Arts, 31
(April 1947), 19, 50 (R).

612. _____. "Wit and the Prat-Fall," Theatre Arts, 31
(April 1947), 19, 49 (All My Sons).

613. Gill, Brendan. "The Creation of the World and Other
Business," New Yorker, 48 (December 9, 1972), 109
(R).

614. _____. "The Crucible," New Yorker, 48 (May 6,
1972), 54 + (R).

615. _____. "An Enemy of the People," New Yorker, 47
(March 20, 1971), 93 (R).

616. _____. "In the Wilderness," New Yorker, 43 (February 17, 1968), 99 (The Price) (R).

617 _____. "The Price," New Yorker, 43 (February 17,
1968), 99 (R).

618. _____. "A View from the Bridge," New Yorker, 37
(January 27, 1962), 82 (FR).

619. Gilman, Richard. "After the Fall," Commonweal, 79
(February 14, 1964), 600-01 (R).

620. _____. "The Drama Is Coming Now," Tulane Drama
Review, 7 (Summer 1963), 27-42.

621. _____. "The Stage," Commonweal, 79 (February 14,
1964), 600-01; Book Week (March 8, 1964), 6, 13 (After
the Fall).

622. _____. "Still Falling," Commonweal, 79 (February
14, 1964), 600-01 (After the Fall).

623. Girson, Rochelle. Saturday Review of Literature, 32

(February 26, 1949), 30; also in 32 (August 13, 1949),
31; 46 (August 24, 1963), 24 (Death of a Salesman).

624. Goldman, Arnold. "I Don't Need You Any More," Listener, 78 (November 2, 1967), 580 (R).

625. Goodman, W. "How Not to Produce a Film," New Republic, 133 (December 26, 1955), 12-13.

626. Grauman, Lawrence, Jr. "The Misfits," Film Quarterly, 14 (Spring 1961), 51-53 (FR).

627. Green, E. M. "All My Sons," Theatre World, 43 (April 1947), 32.

628. Griffin, Alice. "The Crucible," Theatre Arts, 40
(February 1956), 80 (R).

629. Griffin, J. & A. "The Crucible," Theatre Arts, 37
(October 1953), 33-34.

630. Groff, Edward. "A Point of View in Modern Drama,"
Modern Drama, 2 (1959), 268-82 (Death of a Salesman).

631. Gross, Barry Edward. "Peddler and Pioneer in Death
of a Salesman," Modern Drama, 7 (Fall 1965), 405-10.

632. Hagopian, John V. "AM: The Salesman's Two Cases,"
Modern Drama, 6 (September 1963), 117-25 (Death of
Salesman).

633. Hamilton, Jac. "Marilyn's New Life," Life, 21 (October 1, 1957), 110-15.

634. Hamilton, William. "Of God and Woman: The Misfits," Christian Century, 78 (April 5, 1961), 424-25
(FR)

635. Handlin, Oscar. "I Don't Need You Any More," Atlantic, 219 (March 1967), 143 (R).

636. Hanscom, Leslie. "After the Fall: AM's Return,"
Newsweek, 63 (February 3, 1964), 49-52.

637. Hartley, Anthony. "Waterfront," Spectator, 197 (October 19, 1956), 538-40 (A View from the Bridge).

638. Hartley, Arthur. "Good Melodrama," Spectator, 196
      (April 1956), 547 (The Crucible).

639. Hartung, Philip T. "Death of a Salesman," Common-
      weal, 55 (December 28, 1951), 300 (FR).

640. Hartung, Philip T. "The Misfits," Commonweal, 73
      (February 17, 1961), 532-33 (FR).

641. _____. "The Screen," Commonweal, 73 (February
      17, 1961), 532-33 (The Misfits).

642. _____. "A View from the Bridge," Commonweal,
      75 (February 9, 1962), 518-19 (FR).

643. _____. "Witches of Salem," Commonweal, 69 (Janu-
      ary 2, 1959), 363-64 (The Crucible) (FR).

644. Hatch, Robert. "All My Sons: A Matter of Ethics,"
      New Republic, 118 (March 22, 1948), 33 (FR).

645. _____. "Death of a Salesman," New Republic, 125
      (December 31, 1951), 22 (FR).

646. "The Misfits," Nation, 192 (February 18, 1961), 154-
      55 (FR).

647. _____. "A View from the Bridge," Nation, 194
      (February 10, 1962), 125 (FR).

648. Hayes, Richard. "The Stage," Commonweal, 63 (No-
      vember 4, 1955), 117-18 (A Memory of Two Mondays).

649. _____. "The Stage: The Crucible," Commonweal,
      57 (1953), 498; excerpt in A Library of Literary Criti-
      cism, ed. Dorothy Nyren. New York: Ungar, 1960,
      p. 498.

650. _____. "The Stage: I Want My Catharsis," Com-
      monweal, 63 (November 4, 1955), 117-18 (A View from
      the Bridge).

651. Hayman, Ronald. "AM: Between Sartre and Society,"
      Encounter, 37 (November 1971), 73-79.

652. Heaton, C. P. "AM on Death of a Salesman," Notes
      on Contemporary Literature, 1 (January 1971), 5.

653. Heilman, Robert B. "Salesman's Deaths: Documentary
      & Myth," Shenandoah, 20 (1969), 20-8.

654. Hewes, Henry. "AM and How He Went to the Denial,"
      Saturday Review of Literature, 36 (January 31, 1953),
      24-26; excerpt in A Library of Literary Criticism, ed.
      Dorothy Nyren. New York: Ungar, 1960, p. 498 (The
      Crucible); AM, "The Crucible": Text and Criticism,
      ed. Gerald Weales, pp. 182-88.

655. _____. "AM's Cosmic Chuckles," Saturday Review/
      Arts, 1 (January 1973), 57 (The Creation of the World
      and Other Business).

656. _____. "Broadway Postscript," Saturday Review of
      Literature, 47 (December 19, 1964), 24 (Incident at
      Vichy).

657. _____. "Broadway Postscript: Death of a Long-
      shoreman," Saturday Review of Literature, 38 (October
      15, 1955), 25-26 (A View from the Bridge).

658. _____. "Conscience Makes Valiants of Us All,"
      Saturday Review of Literature, 42 (February 21, 1959),
      34 (An Enemy of the People).

659. _____. "The Creation of the World and Other Busi-
      ness," Saturday Review/Arts, 1 (January 1973), 57 (R).

660. _____. "The Crucible," Saturday Review, 55 (May
      20, 1972), 62 (R).

661. _____. "The Price," Saturday Review, 51 (Febru-
      ary 24, 1968), 38 (R).

662. _____. "Quentin's Quest," Saturday Review, 47
      (February 15, 1964), 35 (After the Fall).

663. _____. "Up from Paradise (a dramatic oratorio),"
      Saturday Review/World, 1 (June 15, 1974), 44-47 (R).

664. _____. "Used People," Saturday Review, 51 (Feb-
      ruary 24, 1968), 38 (The Price) (R).

665. _____. "Waiting Periods," Saturday Review, 47
      (December 19, 1964), 24 (Incident at Vichy).

666. _____. "Young Dramatists on Trial in U.S.A.,"
World Theatre, 8 (Autumn 1959), 217-24.

667. Hill, Philip G. "The Crucible: A Structural View,"
Modern Drama, 10 (December 1967), 312-17.

668. Hine, Al. "Death of a Salesman," Holiday, 11 (March
1952), 14 + (FR)

669. Hope-Wallace, P. "Production at Globe Theatre, London," Drama, 10 (Autumn 1958), 11 (All My Sons).

670. _____. "Theatre," Time and Tide, 35 (1954), 1544
(The Crucible).

671. _____. "Theatre: A View from the Bridge," Time
and Tide, 37 (1956), 1267.

672. Hughes, Catherine. "The Creation of the World and
Other Business," America, 127 (December 30, 1972),
570 (R).

673. Hulsopple, Bill G. "Theatre in Southeast Missouri,"
Players Magazine, 36 (February 1960), 106-7 (Southeast Missouri State College uses Cape Girardeau's Theatre to stage AM's The Crucible).

674. Hunt, Albert. "Realism and Intelligence: Some Notes
on AM," Encore (London), 7 (May-June 1960), 12-17,
41; AM, "The Crucible": Text and Criticism, ed. Gerald Weales, pp. 324-32.

675. Hunter, Frederick J. "The Value of Time in Modern
Drama," Journal of Aesthetics & Art Criticism, 16
(1958), 194-201 (Death of a Salesman).

676. Hynes, Joseph A. "AM and the Impasse of Natural-
ism," South Atlantic Quarterly, 62 (1963), 327-34.

677. _____. "Attention Must Be Paid...," College English, 23 (April 1962), 574-78; AM, "Death of a Salesman": Text and Criticism, ed. Gerald Weales, pp.
280-89.

678. "I Don't Need You Any More," Best Sellers, 26 (March
1, 1967), 436 (R).

679. "I Don't Need You Any More," Chicago Sun Book Week,
     February 12, 1967, p. 4 (R).

680. "I Don't Need You Any More," Choice, 4 (July 1967),
     p. 532 (R).

681. "I Don't Need You Any More," Time, 89 (March 10,
     1967), 102 (R).

682. "Incident at Vichy," Booklist, 61 (April 15, 1965), 779
     (R).

683. "Incident at Vichy," Choice, 2 (May 1965), 166 (R).

684. "Incident at Vichy," Life, 58 (January 22, 1965), 39-
     40 (R).

685. "Incident at Vichy," New York Theatre Critics' Re-
     views, 1964, p. 116 (R).

686. "Incident at Vichy," Newsweek, 64 (December 14, 1964),
     86 (R).

687. "Incident at Vichy," Time, 84 (December 11, 1964),
     73 (R).

688. "Innocent and Guilty," Newsweek, 49 (June 10, 1957),
     32.

689. Inserillo, Charles R. "Wish and Desire: Two Poles
     of the Imagination in the Drama of AM and T. S. Eliot,"
     Xavier University Studies, 1 (Spring 1962), 247-58
     (Death of a Salesman).

690. Jackson, Esther Merle. "Death of a Salesman: Tragic
     Myth in the Modern Theatre," CLA Journal, 7 (Septem-
     ber 1963), 63-76.

691. Jacobson, Irving. "Child as Guilty Witness," Litera-
     ture and Psychology, 24 (1974), 12-23.

692. _____. "Family Dreams in Death of a Salesman,"
     American Literature, 47 (May 1975), 247-58.

693. Jaffe, M. "Focus," National Review, 133 (December
     1949), 543-46.

694. James, Stuart B. "Pastoral Dreamer in an Urban
      World," University of Denver Quarterly, 1 (Autumn
      1966), 45-57.

695. Johnson, Gerald W. "Undermining Congress," New
      Republic, 135 (August 6, 1956), 10; (September 10,
      1956), 23. (Reply with rejoinder by Eric Bentley.)

696. Johnson, William. "The Misfits," Modern Photography,
      25 (May 1961), 24-25 (FR).

697. Jones, David E., ed. "A Symposium to Mark the Op-
      ening of the Tyrone Guthrie Repertory Theatre, Minne-
      apolis, Minnesota, May 7, 1963," Drama Survey, 3
      (Spring-Summer 1963), 69-116.

698. Kael, Pauline. "The Innocents and What Passes for
      Experience," Film Quarterly, 15 (1955), 21-36 (A View
      from the Bridge).

699. Kalem, T. E. "Adam and Eve: The Creation of the
      World and Other Business," Time, 100 (December 11,
      1972), 122.

700. _____. "The Crucible," Time, 99 (May 15, 1972),
      59 (R).

701. _____. "An Enemy of the People," Time, 97 (March
      22, 1971), 41 (R).

702. Kalven, Harry, Jr. "A View from the Law," New Re-
      public, 136 (May 27, 1957), 8-13 (A View from the
      Bridge).

703. Kanter, Stefan. "M Plays Variations on 'Salesman,' "
      Life, 64 (March 8, 1968), 18 (The Price).

704. Kass, Robert. "Death of a Salesman," Catholic World,
      174 (February 1952), 386 (FR).

705. Kauffman, Stanley. "Across the Great Divide," New
      Republic, 144 (February 20, 1961), 26, 28 (The Mis-
      fits).

706. _____. "The Misfits," New Republic, 144 (Febru-
      ary 20, 1961), 26 + (FR).

707. _____. "A View from the Bridge," New Republic, 146 (February 12, 1962), 26-27 (FR).

708. Kazan, Elia (Interviewed by Richard Schechner and Theodore Hoffman). "Look There's the American Theatre," Tulane Drama Review, 9 (Winter 1964), 61-83.

709. Keefe, Edward Francis. "Focus," Booklist, 42 (December 1, 1945), 111 (R).

710. _____. "Focus," Commonweal, 43 (December 7, 1945), 219.

711. Kennedy, C. E. "After the Fall: One Man's Look at His Human Nature," Journal of Counseling Psychology, 12 (Summer 1965), 215-17.

712. Kennedy, Leo. "Focus," Chicago Sun Book Week, November 11, 1945, p. 28 (R).

713. Kennedy, Sighle. "Who Killed the Salesman?" Catholic World, 171 (May 1950), 110-16 (Death of a Salesman).

714. Kernodle, George R. "The Death of the Little Man," Tulane Drama Review, 1 (January 1956), 47-60 (Death of a Salesman).

715. Kerr, Walter. "An Enemy of the People," Commonweal, 53 (January 19, 1951), 374.

716. Kilbourn, William. "M: After the Fall," Canadian Forum, 44 (March 1965), 275-76 (An earlier version of this review was broadcast by the CBC on "Viewing the Shows," December 6, 1964).

717. Kirchwey, Freda. "The Crucible," Nation, 176 (February 7, 1953), 131-32; excerpt in A Library of Literary Criticism, ed. Dorothy Nyren. New York: Ungar, 1960, pp. 131-32.

718. Kloten, Edgar. "M in Hartford," Drama Criticism, 11 (1968), 48-9.

719. Knight, Arthur. "A View from the Bridge," Saturday Review, 45 (January 27, 1962), 28 (FR).

720. Koening, Richard E. "The Price," Catholic World, 207 (May 1968), 74-85 (R).

721. Koppenhaver, Allen J. "The Fall and After: Albert Camus and AM," Modern Drama, 9 (September 1966), 206-09.

722. Kostelanetz, Richard. "American Theater--Performance, Not Literature," Re: Arts & Letters, 5 (Fall 1971), 41-49.

723. Kovan, Stanley. "I Don't Need You Any More," Commonweal, 85 (March 17, 1967), 686 (R).

724. Kracht, Fritz Andre. "Rise and Decline of U.S. Theater on German Stages," American-German Review, 22 (June-July 1966), 13-15.

725. Kroll, Jack. "The Creation of the World and Other Business," Newsweek, 80 (December 11, 1972), 71 (R).

726. _____. "The Crucible," Newsweek, 71 (February 19, 1968), 104 (The Price).

727. _____. "An Enemy of the People," Newsweek, 77 (March 22, 1971), 114 (R).

728. _____. "The Price," Newsweek, 71 (February 19, 1968), 104 (R).

729. Krutch, Joseph Wood. "AM Bowdlerizes Ibsen," Nation, 172 (May 5, 1951), 423-24 (An Enemy of the People).

730. _____. "Drama," Nation, 164 (February 15, 1947), 191-93 (All My Sons).

731. _____. "Drama," Nation, 168 (March 5, 1949), 283-84 (Death of a Salesman) (R).

732. Lambert, J. W. "Incident at Vichy," Drama, 80 (Spring 1966), 20-21 (R).

733. Lardner, John. "B for Effort," New Yorker, 22 (February 8, 1947), 50 (All My Sons).

734. Lawrence, S. A. "The Right to Dream in M's Death

of a Salesman," College English, 25 (April 1964), 547-49.

735. Lawson, John Howard. "Modern U.S. Dramaturgy,"
      Inostrannaya Literature (Foreign Literature), 8 (August
      1962), 186-196.

736. Lee, Baxandall, "AM's Latest," Encore, 12 (March-
      April, 1965), 19-23 (After the Fall and Incident at
      Vichy).

737. Leonard, John. "Who's a Misfit? (The Misfits)," Na-
      tional Review, 10 (May 20, 1961), 321-22 (FR).

738. Levin, David. "Salem Witchcraft in Recent Fiction and
      Drama," New England Quarterly, 28 (December 1955),
      537-46; AM, "The Crucible": Text and Criticism, ed.
      Gerald Weales, pp. 248-54.

739. Lewis, Theophilus. "After the Fall," America, 110
      (March 7, 1964), 322 (R).

740. _____. "Incident at Vichy," America, 112 (January
      23, 1965), 147-49 (R).

741. _____. "The Price," America, 118 (March 30, 1968),
      422-3 (R).

742. _____. "A View from the Bridge," America, 44
      (November 19, 1955), 223-24.

743. Leyburn, Ellen Douglas. "Comedy and Tragedy Trans-
      posed," Yale Review, 53 (Summer 1964), 553-62.

744. Loughlin, Richard L. "Tradition and Tragedy in All
      My Sons," English Record, 14 (February 1964), 23-27.

745. McAnany, Emile G. "The Tragic Commitment: Some
      Notes on AM," Modern Drama, 5 (May 1962), 11-20
      (Death of a Salesman).

746. McCalmon, G. "All My Sons," Players Magazine, 25
      (November 1948), 47 (R).

747. McCarten, John. "After the Fall, M on M," New
      Yorker, 30 (February 1, 1964), 59 (R).

748. _____. "All My Sons," New Yorker, 24 (April 3, 1948), 58 (FR).

749. _____. "Death of a Salesman," New Yorker, 27 (December 22, 1951), 70 (FR).

750. _____. "Incident at Vichy," New Yorker, 40 (December 12, 1964), 152 (R).

751. _____. "Witches of Salem (The Crucible)," New Yorker, 34 (December 13, 1958), 110 (FR).

752. McCarthy, Mary. "Americans, Realists, Playwrights," Encounter, 17 (1961), 24-31 (AM, T. Williams, Inge, E. Rice, and O'Neill).

753. _____. "Naming Names: The AM Case," Encounter, 8 (May 1957), 23-25; reprinted in her On the Contrary. New York: Farrar, 1961.

754. _____. " 'Realism' in the American Theatre," Harper's, 223 (July, 1961), 45-52; also as "American, Realists, Playwrights," Encounter, 17 (July, 1961), 24-31.

755. McDonald, Gerald D. "Death of a Salesman," Library Journal, 77 (January 15, 1952), 140 (FR).

756. _____. "A View from the Bridge," Esquire, 57 (February 1962), 22 + (FR).

757. _____. "Witches of Salem (The Crucible)," Library Journal, 84 (January 1, 1959), 70, 88 (FR).

758. Macey, Samuel L. "Non-heroic Tragedy: A Pedigree for American Tragic Drama," Comparative Literature Studies, 6 (March 1969), 1-19.

759. McGraw, William R. "James M. Barrie's Concept of Dramatic Action," Modern Drama, 5 (September 1962), 133-41.

760. McLean, L. "American Weekend: A View of the Country with the AMs," Vogue, 159 (March 15, 1972), 102-109.

761. McMahon, Helen Marie. "AM's Common Man: The

Problem of Realistic and the Mythic," Drama and Theater, 10 (1972), 128-33.

762. "Magnificent Death," Newsweek, 33 (February 21, 1949), 78 (Death of a Salesman).

763. Maini, Darshan Singh. "The Moral Vision of AM," Indian Essays, [n. v.], (1969), 85-96.

764. Malcolm, Donald. "An Enemy of the People," New Yorker, 34 (February 14, 1959), 68, 70 (R).

765. Maloney, Russell. "Situation Normal," Nation, 160 (January 13, 1945), 50 (R).

766. Mannes, M. "Playwright Weds Sex Symbol: Poem," Reporter, 15 (July 12, 1956), 2.

767. "Marilyn's New Life," Look, 21 (October 1, 1959), 110-15.

768. Marshall, Margaret. "Drama," Nation, 172 (January 6, 1951), 18 (An Enemy of the People).

769. Marshall, Thomas F. "A Review of Benjamin Nelson's AM: Portrait of a Playwright," American Literature, 43 (1971), 306-07.

770. Martin, Robert A. "AM & The Meaning of Tragedy," Modern Drama, 13 (1970), 34-39.

771. Mayne, Richard. "The Misfits," New Statesman, 61 (April 28, 1961), 678 (R).

772. "A Memory of Two Mondays," Library Journal, 81 (January 1, 1956), 101 (R).

773. "A Memory of Two Mondays," New York Theatre Critics' Reviews, 1955, p. 272 (R).

774. Meyer, Richard D. and Nancy. "After the Fall: A View from the Director's Notebook," Theatre (Lincoln Center), 2 (1965), 43-73.

775. _____, and _____. "Setting the Stage for Lincoln Center," Theatre Arts, 48 (January 1964), 12-16, 69 (After the Fall).

776. Miller, E. S. "Perceiving and Imagining at Plays,"
     Annali Instituto Universiturio Orientale (Napoli, Sezione
     Germanica), 5 (1963), 5-11.

777. Miller, Jonathan. "After the Fall," Library Journal,
     89 (April 1, 1964), 1620 (R).

778. _____. "After the Fall by AM," New York Review
     of Books, 2 (March 5, 1964), 4.

779. Miller, Jordan Y. "Myth and the American Dream:
     O'Neill to Albee," Modern Drama, 7 (September 1964),
     190-98.

780. "M's Tale," Time, 83 (January 31, 1964), 54.

781. Milton, John R. "The Esthetic Fault of Strindberg's
     'Dream Plays,' " Tulane Drama Review, 4 (March
     1960), 108-16 (After the Fall).

782. "The Misfits," Booklist, 57 (April 15, 1961), 519 (R).

783. "The Misfits," McCall's, 88 (April 1961), 6, 210-11
     (FR).

784. "The Misfits," Time, 77 (February 3, 1961), 68 (FR).

785. "The Misfits: Clark Gable ... Just Before Heart At-
     tack," Life, 49 (November 21, 1900), 06.

786. Monaghan, Charles. "AM as Gnostic," National Re-
     view, 20 (May 21, 1968), 511-12 (The Price).

787. "Morality and Law," Commonweal, 66 (June 14, 1957),
     268-69.

788. Morgan, Frederick. "Notes on the Theatre," Hudson
     Review, 2 (Summer 1949), 272-73; also in The Play:
     A Critical Anthology, ed. Eric Bentley. Englewood
     Cliffs, N.J. : Prentice-Hall, 1962, pp. 746-47 (Death
     of a Salesman).

789. Mortimer, John. "Collected Plays," Encounter, 11
     (October 1958), 87 (R).

790. Moss, Leonard. "AM and the Common Man's Lan-
     guage," Modern Drama, 7 (May 1964), 52-59 (All My

Sons, Death of a Salesman, and The Misfits).

791. _____. "Biographical and Literary Allusion in After
the Fall," Educational Theatre Journal, 17 (December
34-40.

792. Mukerji, Nirmal. "The Proctor's Tragic Predicament,"
Panjab University Research Bulletin, 4 (April 1973),
75-79.

793. Murray, Edward. "A Point of View in After the Fall,"
CLA Journal, 10 (December 1966), 135-42.

794. Nathan, George Jean. "The Crucible," Theatre Arts,
37 (April 1953), 24-26, 65-69.

795. _____, ed. "Tragedy," American Mercury, 68
(June 1949), 679-80 (Death of a Salesman).

796. Nelson, Benjamin. "Avant-Garde Dramatics from Ibsen to Ionesco," Psychoanalytic Review, 55 (1968), 505-
12.

797. Newman, William. "AM's Collected Plays," Twentieth
Century, 164 (November 1958), 491-96; also in Two
Modern American Tragedies, ed. John D. Hurrell.
New York: Scribner's, 1961, pp. 68-71 (R).

798. Nightingale, Benedict. "The Price," New Statesman,
77 (March 14, 1969), 384-85 (R).

799. Nolan, Paul T. "Two Memory Plays: The Glass Menagerie and After the Fall," McNeese Review, 17
(1966), 27-38 (T. Williams and AM).

800. "Notes in Passing," House and Garden, 95 (May 1949),
218, 220 (Death of a Salesman) (R).

801. Novick, Julius. "I at Vichy," Nation, 199 (December
21, 1964), 504 (Incident at Vichy).

802. Oberg, Arthur K. "Death of a Salesman and AM's
Search for Style," Criticism, 9 (1967), 303-11.

803. O'Connor, Frank. "Arctic Arts," Holiday, 19 (February 1956), 65, 68, 70.

804. _____. "The Most American Playwright," Holiday, 19 (February 1956), 65, 68-70.

805. Oliver, Edith. "A View from the Bridge," New Yorker, 40 (February 6, 1965), 94 (R).

806. "One Round for Congress," U.S. News and World Report, 43 (July 5, 1957), 12.

807. Otten, Charlotte F. "Who Am I? A Re-investigation of AM's Death of a Salesman," Cresset, 26 (February 1963), 11-13.

808. "Out of the Fish Bowl," Newsweek, 57 (November 21, 1960), 37.

809. Palmer, Tony. "Artistic Privilege," London Magazine, 8 (April 1968), 47-52 (The Price).

810. Parker, Brian. "Point of View in AM's Death of a Salesman," University of Toronto Quarterly, 35 (1966), 144-57.

811. Parsatharathy, R. "Who's Afraid of Edward Albee? (American Drama in the Sixties)," Quest, 55 (Autumn 1967), 53-55.

812. Payne, Darwin R. "Unit Scenery," Players Magazine, 33 (December 1956), 59, 62 (Southern Illinois University's production of AM's The Crucible and unit scenery).

813. "People," Time, 68 (July 9, 1956), 36.

814. Peterson, Ralph. "Situation Normal," Nation, 160 (January 13, 1945), 50 (R).

815. Phelan, Kappo. "Death of a Salesman," Commonweal, 49 (March 4, 1949), 520-21 (R).

816. _____. "The Stage and Screen: All My Sons," Commonweal, 45 (February 14, 1947), 445-46; also in A Library of Literary Criticism, ed. Dorothy Nyren. New York: Ungar, 1960, pp. 455-46.

817. Phillips, John and Hollander, Anne. "The Art of the Theatre I," Paris Review, 9 (Winter-Spring 1965), 65-

95 (interview with Lillian Hellman). (After the Fall).

818. Pinsker, Sanford. "The End of the Tether: Joseph Conrad's Death of a Salesman," Conradiana, 3 (1971-1972), 74-76 (Conrad and M).

819. "Point of View in After the Fall," College Languages Association Journal, 10 (1966), 135-42.

820. Popkin, Henry. "After the Fall, the Real Shocker," Vogue, 143 (March 15, 1964), 66.

821. _____. "AM Out West," Commentary, 31 (May 1961), 433-36 (The Misfits).

822. _____. "AM: The Strange Encounter," Saturday Review, 68 (Winter 1960), 34-60.

823. _____. "AM's The Crucible," College English, 26 (November 1964), 139-46.

824. _____. "I at Vichy, Needs Something More," Vogue, 145 (January 15, 1965), 27 (Incident at Vichy).

825. _____. "The Misfits," Commentary, 31 (May 1961), 433-36 (FR).

826. "Popsie and Poopsie," Time, 76 (November 21, 1960), 61.

827. Price, Jonathan R. "AM: Fall or Rise," Drama, 73 (Summer 1964), 39-40 (The Crucible, After the Fall, and Death of a Salesman).

828. "The Price," Booklist, 52 (January 15, 1956), 205 (R).

829. "The Price," Life, 64 (March 8, 1968), 18 (R).

830. "The Price," Time, 91 (February 16, 1968), 76-77 (R).

831. Prideaux, Tom. "After the Fall," Life, 56 (February 7, 1964), 64B-64D (R).

832. _____. "A Desperate Search by a Troubled Hero," Life, 56 (February 7, 1964), 64A-65 (After the Fall) (photos by Inge Morath).

833. Prudhoe, John. "AM and the Tradition of Tragedy," English Studies, 43 (October 1962), 430-39.

834. "Pulitzer Prizes Announced by Columbia University," Publishers' Weekly, 155 (May 7, 1949), 1877.

835. Raines, M. B. "The Price," Library Journal, 93 (April 15, 1968), 1649 (R).

836. Raja, Baldev. "AM's After the Fall--A Study in Quest of Innocence," Perspective, [n.v.] (1970), 394-407.

837. Reed, Edward. "Portents in Books: A Year of Theatre Publishing," Theatre Arts, 31 (April 1947), 49-50 (All My Sons).

838. Reno, Raymond H. "AM and the Death of God," Texas Studies in Literature and Language, 11 (Summer 1969), 1069-87.

839. Rey, John B. "Paul Claudel's American Drama," Drama Critique, 4 (May 1961), 73-76.

840. Richardson, Jack. "AM's Eden: The Creation of the World and Other Business," Commentary, 55 (February 1973), 83-85 (R).

841 _____. "Theatre Chronicle," Commentary, 45 (Appril, 1968), 74-76 (The Price) (R).

842. Robotham, J. S. "In Russia with Inge Morath," Library Journal, 95 (February 1, 1970), 496 (R).

843. Rogoff, Gordon. "After the Fall," Nation, 198 (February 10, 1964), 153-54 (R).

844. Rolo, Charles. "The Misfits," Atlantic, 207 (March 1961), 115 (R).

845. Ronald, Margaret Loftus. "Death of a Salesman: Fifteen Years After," Comment, 6 (August 1965), 28-35.

846. Ross, George. "Death of a Salesman in the Original," Commentary, 11 (February 1951), 184-86; AM, Death of a Salesman": Text and Criticism, ed. Gerald Weales, pp. 259-64.

847. Roth, Martin. "Sept-d'un-coup," Chicago Review, 19
     (1966), 108-11 (Incident at Vichy).

848. Rothenberg, Albert and Shapiro, Eugene D. "The De-
     fense of Psychoanalysis in Literature: Long Day's
     Journey into Night and A View from the Bridge," Com-
     parative Drama, 7 (1973), 51-67.

849. Rovere, Richard H. "AM's Conscience," New Republic,
     (June 7, 1957), 13-15; excerpt in A Library of Literary
     Criticism, ed. Dorothy Nyren. New York: Ungar,
     1960, p. 13; AM, "The Crucible": Text and Criticism,
     ed. Gerald Weales, pp. 315-23.

850. _____. "Monroe Doctrine," Spectator, 196 (June 29,
     1956), 877.

851. Russell, Robert. "Gawd Those Jokes Were Painful,"
     Esquire, 70 (December 1968), 164-69.

852. Saisselin, Remy G. "Is Tragic Drama Possible in the
     20th Century?" Theatre Annual, 17 (1960), 12-21
     (Death of a Salesman).

853. Sanche, Don A. "We Call on The Saturday Evening
     Post," Esquire, 72 (November 1969), 40+.

854. "Scene (Picture) from Production By Company of Four,
     London," Theatre World, 45 (December 1949), 24 (All
     My Sons).

855. Schneider, Daniel E. "Play of Dreams," Theatre Arts,
     33 (October 1949), 18-21; excerpt in A Library of Lit-
     erary Criticism, ed. Dorothy Nyren. New York: Un-
     gar, 1960, pp. 18-21 (Death of a Salesman).

856. Schraepen, Edmond. "AM's Constancy: A Note on M
     as a Short Story Writer," Revue des Langues Vivantes,
     36 (1970), 62-71.

857. Schweinitz, G. D. "Death of a Salesman: A Note on
     Epic and Tragedy," Western Humanities Review, 14
     14 (Winter 1960), 91-96.

858. Seager, Allan. "The Creative Agony of M," Esquire,
     52 (October 1959), 23-26; AM, "Death of a Salesman":
     Text and Criticism, ed. Gerald Weales, pp. 326-38.

859. Selz, Jean. "Raymond Rouleau Among the Witches," tr. by Gerald Weales, Les Lettres Nouvelles, 3 (March 1955), 422-26; AM, "The Crucible": Text and Criticism, ed. & tr. Gerald Weales, pp. 242-47.

860. Shatzsky, Joel. "The 'Reactive Image' and M's Death of a Salesman," Players, 48 (1973), 104-10.

861. Shea, Albert A. "Death of a Salesman," Bookmark, 9 (October 1949), 4 (R).

862. _____. "Death of a Salesman," Canadian Forum, 29 (July 1949), 86-87; excerpt in A Library of Literary Criticism, ed. Dorothy Nyren. New York: Ungar, 1960, pp. 86-89.

863. Sheed, Wilfrid. "Revival of a Salesman," Commonweal, 81 (February 19, 1965), 670-71 (Death of a Salesman).

864. _____. "The Stage," Commonweal, 81 (February 19, 1965), 670-71 (Death of a Salesman).

865. _____. "A View from the Bridge," Commonweal, 81 (February 19, 1965), 670 (R).

866. Sheffer, Isaiah. "I Don't Need You Any More," New Leader, 50 (June 5, 1967), 23 (R).

867. Shepherd, Allen. " 'What Comes Easier': The Short Stories of AM," Illinois Quarterly, 34 (February 1972), 37-49.

868. Shipley, Joseph T. "AM's New Melodrama Is Not What It Seems to Be," New Leader, 36 (February 9, 1953), 25-26; AM, "The Crucible": Text and Criticism, ed. Gerald Weales, pp. 201-03.

869. Siegel, Paul N. "The Drama and the Thwarted American Dream," Lock Haven Review, 7 (1965), 52-62 (Death of a Salesman).

870. _____. "Willy Loman and King Lear," College English, 17 (March 1956), 341-45 (Death of a Salesman).

871. Simon, John. "The Price," Commonweal, 87 (March 1, 1968), 655 (R).

872. _____. "Settling the Account," Commonweal, 87
(March 1, 1968), 655 (The Price).

873. _____. "Theatre Chronicle," Hudson Review, 17
(Summer 1964), 234-36 (After the Fall) (R).

874. _____. "The Tragedy of American Theatre: AM,"
Holiday, 39 (March 1966), 76 +.

875. "Situation Normal," Booklist, 41 (January 1, 1945),
133 (R).

876. "Sketch, Portrait," Time, 53 (February 21, 1949), 74-
75.

877. Small, Christopher. "Theatre," Spectator, 193 (November 19, 1954), 608 (The Crucible).

878. Smith, Harrison. "Focus," New Yorker, 21 (November 3, 1945), 102 (R).

879. _____. "Focus by AM," Saturday Review of Literature, 38 (November 7, 1945), 11.

880. _____. "The Shape of a Human Face," Saturday Review of Literature, 28 (November 17, 1945), 11 (Focus).

881. Sommers, Florence. "A View from the Bridge," Redbook, 118 (February 1962), 29 (FR).

882. Sontag, Susan. "After the Fall," Partisan Review, 31
(Spring 1964), 284-87 (R).

883. Spiller, Robert E. "All My Sons," Theatre Arts, 31
(April 1947), 50 (FR).

884. Stallknecht, Newton P., et al. "Symposium: Death of
a Salesman," Folio (Indiana University), 17 (March
1952), 3-26.

885. Standley, Fred L. "An Echo of Milton in The Crucible,"
N & Q, 15 (August 1968), 303.

886. Steene, Birgitta. "AM's After the Fall," Moderna
Sprak, 58 (1964), 446-52.

887. _____. "The Critical Reception of American Drama

in Sweden," <u>Modern Drama,</u> 5 (May 1962), 71-82.

888. Steinbeck, John.   "The Trial of AM," <u>Esquire</u>, 47 (June 1957), 86.

889. _____. "The Trial of AM; Reprint from June 1957 Issue," <u>Esquire</u>, 80 (October 1973), 238-240.

890. Steinberg, M. W.   "AM and the Idea of Modern Tragedy," <u>Dalhousie Review,</u> 40 (Autumn 1960), 329-40.

891. Stevens, Virginia.   "Seven Young Broadway Artists," <u>Theatre Arts</u>, 31 (June 1947), 53-56.

892. _____. "Sketch, Portrait," <u>Theatre Arts,</u> 31 (June 1947), 52, 56.

893. Stinson, John J.   "Structure in <u>After the Fall</u>: The Relevance of the Maggie Episodes to the Main Themes and the Christian Symbolism," <u>Modern Drama,</u> 10 (December 1967), 233-40.

894. <u>The Story of G. I. Joe,</u> a filmscript, based on material contained in Ernie Pyle's <u>Here Is Your War</u>, selected by M, scripted by Leopold Atlas, Guy Endore, and Philip Stevenson.   <u>Theatre Arts,</u> 29 (September 1945), 514-21.

895. Streiker, Lowell D.   "Sons and Brothers," <u>Christian Century</u>, 85 (March 27, 1968), 405-06 (<u>The Price</u>) (R).

896. Sylvester, Robert.   "Brooklyn Boy Makes Good," <u>Saturday Evening Post</u>, 222 (July 16, 1949), 26-27, 97-98, 100.

897. Therese, Sister Marian.   "M in Princeton," <u>Drama Criticism,</u> 11 (1968), 49-51.

898. Thomas, Miles O.   "Three Authors in Search of a Character," <u>Personalist,</u> 46 (Winter 1965), 65-72 (Albert Camus, Aldous Huxley, and AM).

899. Thompson, Alan.   "Professor's Debauch," <u>Theatre Arts</u>, 35 (March 1951), 25-27.

900. Thompson, C.   "New York's Communist Cop: Ex-Policeman," <u>Saturday Evening Post</u>, 226 (March 20,

1954), 19 +.

901. Trauber, Shepard. "Drama," Nation, 181 (October 22, 1955), 348-49 (A View from the Bridge).

902. Trewin, J. C. "Blanket of the Dark," Illustrated London News, 225 (November 27, 1954), 964 (The Crucible).

903. _____. "A View from the Bridge," Illustrated London News, 229 (October 27, 1956), 720 (R).

904. _____. "The World of the Theatre," Illustrated London News, 229 (October 27, 1956), 720 (A View from the Bridge).

905. Trowbridge, C. W. "AM: Between Pathos and Tragedy," Modern Drama, 10 (December 1967), 221-32.

906. Tynan, Kenneth. "American Blues: The Plays of AM and Tennessee Williams," Encounter, 2 (May 1954), 13-19; also in his Curtains. New York: Atheneum, 1961, pp. 257-66.

907. Van Rensselaer, Euphemia See Wyatts, Euphemia Van Rensselaer (966).

908. "A View from the Bridge," Life, 39 (October 17, 1955), 166-67.

909. "A View from the Bridge," New York Theatre Critics' Reviews, 1955, p. 272 (R).

910. "A View from the Bridge," Newsweek, 59 (January 22, 1962), 80-81 (FR).

911. "A View from the Bridge," Newsweek, 65 (March 15, 1965), 93 (R).

912. "A View from the Bridge," Theatre Arts, 39 (December 1955), 18-19; 41 (May 1957), 28-29.

913. "A View from the Bridge," Time, 66 (October 10, 1955), 53 (R).

914. "A View from the Bridge," Time, 79 (January 19, 1962), 55 (R).

915. "A View from the Bridge," Twentieth Century, 161 (January 1957), 56-62 (R).

916. "A View from the Bridge," Vogue, 145 (August 15, 1965), 56 (R).

917. Vos, Nelvin. "The American Dream Turned Nightmare: Recent American Drama," Christian Scholar's Review, 1 (Spring 1971), 195-206.

918. Wakeman, John. "I Don't Need You Any More," Library Journal, 92 (February 1, 1967), 596 (R).

919. Walker, Philip. "AM's The Crucible; Tragedy or Allegory?" Western Speech, 20 (1956), 222-24.

920. Walsh, Moira. "The Misfits," America, 104 (February 18, 1961), 676 + (FR).

921. _____. "The Witches of Salem," America, 100 (January 17, 1959), 480-82 (The Crucible) (FR).

922. Warshow, Robert. "Death of a Salesman," Commentary, 13 (March 1952), 275. 81 (FR).

923. _____. "The Liberal Conscience in The Crucible," Commentary, 15 (March 1953), 265-71; also in The Scene Before You: A New Approach to American Culture, ed. Charles Brossard. New York. Rinehart, 1955, pp. 191-203; rep. by Stanley Rothman and Bernard Marcus with rejoinder by Robert Warshow, Commentary, 16 (July 1953), 83-84.

924. Weales, Gerald. "All about Talk: AM's The Price," Ohio Review, 13 (1972), 74-84.

925. _____. "American Drama Since the Second World War," Tamarack Review, 13 (Autumn, 1959), 86-99.

926. _____. "AM: Man and His Image," Tulane Drama Review, 7 (September 1962), 165-80; also in American Drama Since World War II, by Gerald Weales. New York: Harcourt, 1962.

927. _____. "AM's Collected Plays," Commonweal, 66 (July 12, 1957), 382-83.

928. _____. "Collected Plays," Bookmark, 16 (June 1957), 211 (R).

929. _____. "Collected Plays," Commonweal, 66 (July 12, 1957), 382 (R).

930. _____. "The Creation of the World and Other Business," Commonweal, 97 (December 22, 1972), 276 (R).

931. _____. "The Misfits," Reporter, 24 (March 2, 1961), 46-47 (FR).

932. _____. "Plays and Analysis," Commonweal, 66 (July 12, 1957), 382-83 (A View from the Bridge).

933. _____. "The Price," Reporter, 38 (March 21, 1968), 42, 44 (R).

934. _____. "The Song of Solomon," Reporter, 38 (March 21, 1968), 42 + (The Price).

935. _____. "Tame and Wooly West," Reporter, 24 (March 2, 1961), 46-47 (The Misfits).

936. Weatherby, W. J. "The Misfits: Epic or Requiem?" Saturday Review of Literature, 44 (February 4, 1961), 26-27.

937. Webster, Margaret. "A View from the Bridge," Theatre Arts, 41 (May 1957), 28-29 (R).

938. "Wedding Wine for Marilyn," Life, 41 (July 16, 1956), 113-15.

939. Wells, Arvin R. "All My Sons," Insight I, Frankfurt: Hirschgroben, 1962, pp. 165-74. Reprinted in revised form as "The Living and the Dead in All My Sons," Modern Drama, 7 (1964), 46-51.

940. _____. "The Living and the Dead in All My Sons," Modern Drama, 7 (1964), 46-51.

941. West, Paul. "AM and the Human Mice," Hibbert Journal, 61 (January 1963), 84-86.

942. Weyergans, Franz. "AM's The Misfits," Revue Nouvelle, 33 (June 1961), 668-72.

943. "When Silence Is Contempt of Congress," U.S. News
and World Report, 42 (July 7, 1957), 14.

944. Whitcomb, J. "Marilyn Monroe ... the Sex Symbol
versus the Good Wife," Cosmopolitan, 149 (December
1960), 53-57.

945. _____. "Our Location," Cosmopolitan, 149 (December 1960), 52-57.

946. White, W. R. "Death of a Salesman," New Yorker,
25 (May 21, 1949), 117 (R).

947. Whitcbait, William. "All My Sons," New Statesman
and Nation, 36 (September 4, 1948), 193 (FR).

948. _____. "Witches of Salem (The Crucible)," New
Statesman, 54 (September 7, 1957), 276 + (FR).

949. Whitley, Alvin. "AM: An Attempt at Modern Tragedy," Transactions of the Wisconsin Academy of Sciences, Arts, and Letters, 42 (1953), 257-62.

950. Wiegand, William. "AM and the Man Who Knows,"
Western Review, 21 (Winter 1957), 85-103; AM, "Death
of a Salesman": Text and Criticism, ed. Gerald
Weales, pp. 290-312; AM, "The Crucible": Text and
Ciiticism, ed. Gerald Weales, pp. 290-314.

951. Willett, Ralph W. "The Ideas of M and Williams,"
Theatre Annual, 22 (1965-66), 31-40.

952. _____. "A Note on AM's The Price," Journal of
American Studies, 5 (December 1971), 307-10.

953. Williams, Raymond. "The Realism of AM," Critical
Quarterly, 1 (Summer 1959), 140-49; AM, "Death of a
Salesman": Text and Criticism, ed. Gerald Weales,
pp. 313-25.

954. Willis, Robert J. "AM's The Crucible: Relevant for
All Times," Faculty Journal (East Stroudsburg [Pa.]
State College), 1 (1970), 5-14.

955. Wilson, Colin. "The Winter and Publicity: A Reply to
Critics," Encounter, 13 (November 1959), 8-13.

956. Winegarten, Renee. "The World of AM," Jewish Quarterly, 17 (Summer 1969), 48-53.

957. "Witches of Salem (The Crucible)," Time, 73 (January 5, 1959), 84 (FR).

958. Worsley, T. C. "American Tragedy," New Statesman, 56 (August 23, 1958), 220.

959. _____. "AM's The Crucible," New Statesman and Nation, 51 (April 14, 1956), 370-71.

960. _____. "A Play of Our Time," New Statesman and Nation, 48 (November 20, 1954), 642 (The Crucible).

961. _____. "Poetry Without Words," New Statesman and Nation, 38 (August 6, 1949), 146-47; AM, "Death of a Salesman": Text and Criticism, ed. Gerald Weales, pp. 224-27.

962. _____. "Realistic Melodrama," New Statesman and Nation, 52 (October 20, 1956), 482 (A View from the Bridge).

963. _____. "The Theatre," New Statesman and Nation, 35 (May 22, 1948), 412 (All My Sons).

964. _____. "A View from the Bridge," New Statesman and Nation, 52 (October 20, 1956), 482 (R).

965. Wyatt, Euphemia Van Rensselaer. "Theater," Catholic World, 164 (March 1947), 552-53 (All My Sons) (R).

966. _____. "Theater," Catholic World, 169 (April 1949), 62 (Death of a Salesman) (R).

967. _____. "Theatre," Catholic World, 172 (February 1951), 387 (An Enemy of the People) (R).

968. _____. "Theatre," Catholic World, 176 (March 1953), 465-66 (The Crucible) (R).

969. _____. "Theatre," Catholic World, 182 (November 1955), 144-45 (A View from the Bridge) (R).

970. Yorks, Samuel A. "Joe Keller and His Sons," Western Humanities Review, 13 (Autumn 1959) 401-07. (All My Sons).

971. Young, Stark. "Theatre: Good Occasion," <u>New Re-</u>
      <u>public</u>, 116 (February 10, 1947), 42; excerpt in <u>A Li-</u>
      <u>brary of Literary Criticism</u>, ed. Dorothy Nyren (<u>All</u>
      <u>My Sons</u>).

972. Zimmerman, Paul. "<u>I Don't Need You Any More</u>,"
      <u>New York Times Book Review</u>, April 2, 1967, p. 4
      (R).

973. _____. "<u>I Don't Need You Any More</u>," <u>Newsweek</u>,
      69 (February 27, 1967), 92 (R).

7. NEWSPAPER ARTICLES, REVIEWS, AND REPORTS

974. "A. Clurman Quits as Director of The Creation of the World and Other Business," New York Times, October 17, 1972, p. 35:2.

975. "A. Einstein College of Medicine Selects Names of 1973 Recipients of A. Einstein Commemorative Awards; Winners Include AM," New York Times, May 4, 1973, p. 27:1.

976. "After the Fall," New York Theatre Critics' Reviews, 1964, p. 374 (R).

977. "After the Fall," Times (London) Literary Supplement, February 4, 1965, p. 89 (R).

978. "After the Fall: English-Language Production, Paris, Unsuccessful 1965 French-Language Production Noted," New York Times, February 1, 1966, p. 26:1.

979. "After the Fall: M to Withdraw Play from Lincoln Center Repertory in June in Wake of Dispute at Center," New York Times, January 1, 1965, X:3.

980. "After the Fall, or The Survivor: Author Reads Play at Lincoln Center Repertory Theater First Rehearsal," New York Times, October 25, 1963, p. 29:3.

981. "After the Fall: Saturday Evening Post to Publish Play," New York Times, January 11, 1964, p. 15:2.

982. "All My Sons," New York Theatre Critics' Reviews, 1947, p. 475 (R).

983. "All My Sons," San Francisco Chronicle, May 18, 1947, p. 20 (R).

984. "All My Sons, a Hit: London Critic Calls Drama Best

Serious Play from America," New York Times, May 12, 1948, p. 33:3.

985. "All My Sons: Circuit Court, Milford, Conn. Rejects Citizens Anti-Communist Committee Complaint That Sunday Performance at United Church of Christ Violates Sunday Observance Law," New York Times, November 10, 1961, p. 11:1.

986. "All My Sons: The Manuscript Will be Sold at Auction," New York Times, May 14, 1947, p. 31:3.

987. "All My Sons to Be Staged in Moscow," New York Times, October 18, 1949, p. 34:4.

988. "American Academy of Arts and Letters Election, 6 Members Named," New York Times, December 9, 1971, p. 59:3.

989. "American Academy of Arts and Letters Gold Medal Goes to AM," New York Times, January 28, 1959, p. 21:5.

990. "American Bar Association Committee Chairman Sidlo Assails Lines Disparaging Lawyers, Letter to Martin Beck Theatre; M replies; Refuses to Make Change; Sidlo Comments," New York Times, March 9, 1953, I, 3 (The Crucible).

991. "American Civil Liberties' Union New York Chapter Scores Probe of M," New York Times, October 26, 1955, I, 2.

992. "American Committee for Cultural Freedom Challenges USSR Writers Union to Publicize M Statement; Radio Liberation to Beam Excerpt to USSR," New York Times, February 15, 1956, p. 28:6.

993. "American Committee for Cultural Freedom Welcomes Criticism, But Denies It Solicited Comments; M's Reply; Committee Scores Him for Comparing Situation in USSR and US; M's Reply," New York Times, February 14, 1956, p. 5:1.

994. "American Cultural Freedom Committee Chairman Farrell's Letter on M's Views Marking Anniversary of the Death of Dostoevsky," New York Times, February 21, 1956, p. 32:6.

995.   "American Jewish Congressional Women's Division
        Criticizes Secretary Dulles for Curbs on Americans,"
        New York Times, May 9, 1957, p. 3:5.

996.   "AM and Brazilian Director A. Boal Meet in NYC,"
        New York Times, June 25, 1971, p. 16:1.

997.   "AM and Rev. W. S. Coffin Urge Support of E. Mc-
        Carthy," New York Times, March 3, 1968, p. 78:1.

998.   "AM and Yale Chaplain Coffin for E. McCarthy, New
        Haven, Conn." New York Times, March 3, 1968,
        p. 78:1.

999.   "AM Appointed Adjunct Professor-in-Residence at Ann
        Arbor Campus of the University of Michigan," New
        York Times, July 31, 1973, p. 34:1.

1000.   "AM, Author of Death of a Salesman Agrees to Allow
        Philadelphia Drama Guild to Perform Work; Had
        Previously Refused to Allow Professional Production
        of Play either in NYC or in Any Place Within 100
        Miles of Broadway," New York Times, November 4,
        1973, p. 83:1.

1001.   "AM Comments on Significance of 1st Manned Lunar
        Landing," New York Times, July 21, 1969, p. 7.

1002.   "AM Comments, Plans Appeal to USSR and Soviet
        Writers Union," New York Times, August 31, 1968,
        p. 1:2.

1003.   "AM Fined; Plans an Appeal," New York Times, July
        20, 1957, p. 4:3.

1004.   "AM Has Granted Permission to University Players of
        University of Michigan to Perform Scenes Next Spring
        from His Incompleted Play, The American Clock,"
        New York Times, September 9, 1973, p. 58:1.

1005.   "AM Hopes His Refusal to Allow His Recent Plays to
        be Published in Greece Will Spur U.S. Intellectual
        Community to Campaign for End to U.S. Aid," New
        York Times, July 3, 1969, p. 29:1.

1006.   "AM Illustration," New York Times, February 15,
        1969, p. 20:2.

1007. "AM Illustration," New York Times, November 17, 1969, p. 58:1.

1008. "AM Offers Resolution Calling for Bombing Cessation," New York Times, June 22, 1968, p. 19:4.

1009. "AM on Senator McGovern," Times (London), November 6, 1972, p. 12 e.

1010. "AM Portrait," New York Times, May 18, 1970, p. 28:2.

1011. "AM Publishes Critical Account of Soviet Literary Policies in Harper's," New York Times, August 17, 1969, p. 26:2.

1012. "AM Recent Re-election as PEN International President," New York Times, May 9, 1967, p. 44:3.

1013. "AM Refuses Bid by 3 Greek Publishers to Publish His Play The Price and Other of His Works," New York Times, July 3, 1969, p. 29:1.

1014. "AM Said Ginsberg's Publications Were on Level with National Geographic," New York Times, February 18, 1972, p. 16:4.

1015. "AM Says He Will Urge PEN to Debate Kuznetsov Defection, and His Articles on Soviet Censorship and Repression," New York Times, August 12, 1969, p. 36:7.

1016. "AM Sees Basic Problem of Broadway Theater Economic," New York Times, December 21, 1969, II, 3:1.

1017. "AM Signs Statement Protesting Teacher's Suspension," New York Times, February 23, 1970, p. 24:2.

1018. "AM Writes Critical Account of USSR Literary Scene," New York Times, August 17, 1969, p. 26:1.

1019. "AM's The Price," Times Literary Supplement, October 10, 1968, p. 1154.

1020. Atkinson, Brooks. "All My Sons," New York Times, January 30, 1947, p. 21:2 (R).

1021. _____. "All My Sons," New York Times, February 9, 1947, II, 1:1 (R).

1022. _____. "All My Sons," New York Times, September 7, 1947, II, 1:4 (R).

1023. _____. "Arthur Kennedy's The Crucible in a New Edition," New York Times, July 2, 1953, p. 20:2 (R).

1024. _____. "AM's The Crucible in a New Edition with Several New Actors and One New Scene," New York Times, July 2, 1953, p. 20:2; AM, "The Crucible": Text and Criticism, ed. Gerald Weales, pp. 194-96.

1025. "AM's Tragedy of an Ordinary Man: Death of a Salesman," New York Times, February 20, 1949, II, 1:1 (R).

1026. _____. "At the Theatre," New York Times, January 23, 1953, p. 15; AM, "The Crucible": Text and Criticism, ed. Gerald Weales, pp. 192-94 (R).

1027. _____. "The Crucible," New York Times, January 23, 1953, p. 15:3 (R).

1028. _____. "The Crucible," New York Times, February 1, 1953, II, 1:1 (R); March 15, 1953, II, 1:1 (R).

1029. _____. "The Crucible," New York Times, March 12, 1958, p. 21:1 (R).

1030. _____. "The Crucible," New York Times, June 1, 1958, II, 1:1.

1031. _____. "Death of a Salesman," New York Times, February 11, 1949, p. 27:2; also in The Play: A Critical Anthology, ed. Eric Bentley. New York: Prentice-Hall, 1962, pp. 729 & 731 (R).

1032. _____. "Death of a Salesman," New York Times, February 20, 1949, II, 1; also in Two Modern American Tragedies, ed. John D. Hurrell. New York: Scribner's, 1961, pp. 54-56 (R).

1033. _____. "Death of a Salesman," New York Times, March 12, 1950, II, 1:1 (R).

1034. _____. "Death of a Salesman," New York Times,
May 15, 1949, II, 1:1-3 (R).

1035. _____. "Death of a Salesman: T. Mitchell Interpretation of Role Reviewed," New York Times, September 21, 1950, p. 20:5 (R).

1036. _____. "An Enemy of the People," New York
Times, January 7, 1951, II, 1:1 (R).

1037. _____. "Five by M," New York Times, June 9,
1957, II, p. 1.

1038. _____. "Frederic March in An Enemy of the People," New York Times, December 29, 1950, p. 14:1
(R).

1039. _____. "A Memory of Two Mondays," New York
Times, September 30, 1955, p. 21:1 (R).

1040. _____. "A Memory of Two Mondays," New York
Times, October 9, 1955, II, 1:1 (R).

1041. _____. "M's Ibsen: An Enemy of the People,"
New York Times, February 5, 1958, p. 24:4 (R).

1042. _____. "Thomas Mitchell Brings His Portrait of
Willy Loman to the Morosco," New York Times,
September 21, 1950, p. 20:5 (Death of a Salesman)
(R).

1043. _____. "A View from the Bridge," New York
Times, October 9, 1955, I, 1 (R).

1044. _____. "A View from the Bridge: AM's Two
Short Plays Staged," New York Times, September 30,
1955, p. 21:1 (R).

1045. Barnes, Clive. "AM's The Creation Directed by Harold Clurman Who Quits as Director," New York
Times, December 1, 1972, p. 28:1.

1046. _____. "AM's The Price," New York Times,
February 8, 1968, p. 37:1 (R).

1047. _____. "The Creation of the World and Other
Business," New York Times, Dec. 1, 1972, p. 28:1
(R).

1048. _____. "Lincoln Center Presents AM Version,"
New York Times, March 12, 1971, p. 26:1 (Enemy
of the People).

1049. _____. "NYC Production of The Price Reap-
praised," New York Times, October 30, 1968, p.
39:2 (R).

1050. _____. "The Price," New York Times, February
8, 1968, p. 37:1 (R).

1051. _____. "Reappraisal of AM's The Price," New
York Times, October 30, 1968, p. 39:1 (R).

1052. _____. "Stage: M's The Crucible," New York
Times, April 28, 1972, p. 36:1 (R).

1053. Barry, Iris. "Focus," New York Herald Tribune,
November 18, 1945, p. 4 (R).

1054. "Bars Data on M Romance with M. Monroe," New
York Times, May 22, 1957, p. 17:3.

1055. Basseches, Maurice. "Situation Normal," New York
Times, December 24, 1944, p. 3 (R).

1056. Beaufort, John. "Death of a Salesman," Christian
Science Monitor, March 5, 1949, p. 12 (R).

1057. Bermel, Albert. "Right, Wrong and Mr. M," New
York Times, April 14, 1968, II, 1 & 7.

1058. "Bondin and Bick Committee Orders M to Answer
Queries on Communist-Front Associations or Face
Contempt Citation; Seeks Data on 1954 Passport Deni-
al and Current Passport Application; Votes Contempt
Proceedings against Nathan," New York Times, June
28, 1956, p. 10:3.

1059. "Both American Groups (American Committee for Cul-
tural Freedom and for Liberation from Bolshevism)
Dare USSR to Publicize M Statement," New York
Times, February 15, 1956, p. 28:6.

1060. "Brandeis University Creative Arts Awards Medals
and Citations Presented to 8 Persons," New York
Times, May 18, 1970, p. 38:1.

1061. Breit, Harvey. "Death of a Salesman: Thomas Mann Comments," New York Times Book Review, May 29, 1949, VII, 2:2-4.

1062. "Brooks Atkinson on His Collected Plays," New York Times, June 9, 1957, II, 1:1 (R).

1063. Brown, Ivor. "As London Sees Willy Loman," New York Times Magazine, August 28, 1949, VI, II & 59 (R); also in The Play: A Critical Anthology, ed. Eric Bentley. Englewood Cliffs, N. J.: Prentice-Hall, 1962, pp. 732-36; AM, "Death of a Salesman": Text and Criticism, ed. Gerald Weales, pp. 244-49.

1064. _____. "Death of a Salesman," New York Times, August 28, 1949, VI, 11:1 (R).

1065. Brown, John Mason. "The Crucible," San Francisco Chronicle, October 4, 1953, p. 22 (R).

1066. _____. "Death of a Salesman," San Francisco Chronicle, May 22, 1949, p. 19 (R).

1067. Buckley, Tom. "In the Beginning, M's The Creation," New York Times, December 5, 1972, p. 49:1; p. 67: 4.

1068. _____. "M Takes His Comedy [The Creation of the World and Other Business] Seriously," New York Times, August 29, 1972, p. 22:1.

1069. Burg, Victor. "In Russia with Inge Morath," Christian Science Monitor, January 8, 1970, p. 17 (R).

1070. Butterfield, Alfred. "Focus," New York Times Book Review, November 18, 1945, p. 15 (R).

1071. Calta, Louis. "Comments on The Creation of the World and Other Business," New York Times, May 19, 1972, p. 19:1.

1072. _____. "The Creation of the World and Other Business," New York Times, October 17, 1972, p. 35:1 (R).

1073. _____. "Comments on The Creation of the World and Other Business," New York Times, May 19,

1972, p. 19:1 (R).

1074. "Career; Illustrated with Wife, New York Times, June 1, 1957, p. 8:4.

1075. Coe, Richard L. "Revised Bridge Given in Capital Arena Stage Offers M's Waterfront Drama in New Hospitality Hall Home," New York Times, November 9, 1956, p. 34.

1076. "Collected Plays," San Francisco Chronicle, June 2, 1957, p. 24 (R).

1077. "Collected Plays," Times (London) Literary Supplement, August 29, 1958, p. 482 (R).

1078. "Comment," New York Times, February 1, 1953, II, 1:1 (The Crucible) (R).

1079. "Comment on AM's Dec. 23 Essay," New York Times, December 30, 1967, p. 22:5.

1080. "Connecticut and National Committee Chairman Bailey Names P. Newman and AM to State Delegation," New York Times, July 10, 1968, p. 43:3.

1081. Cook, Jim. "Their Thirteenth Year Was the Most Significant," Washington Post & Times Herald, July 10, 1956, p. 24.

1082. Corry, John. "National Institute of Arts and Letters: AM as One of the Newly-Elected Members," New York Times, May 18, 1972, p. 49:1.

1083. "Court Re-Affirms M Conviction, But Drops One Count in Light of Watkins Case Decision; One Count against Nathan also Dismissed," New York Times, June 29, 1957, p. 4:4.

1084. "The Creation of the World and Other Business by AM to Be Produced on Broadway," New York Times, September 9, 1971, p. 50:4.

1085. "The Creation of the World and Other Business Closes on December 16 After 20 Performances," New York Times, December 17, 1972, II 5:6.

1086.   "The Creation of the World and Other Business Dis-
        cussed," New York Times, October 3, 1971, II, 1:3
        (R).

1087.   "The Creation of the World and Other Business Is
        Scheduled to Close on December 16 after 20 Per-
        formances," New York Times, December 8, 1972,
        p. 37:2.

1088.   "The Creation of the World and Other Business Opens
        on November 30, 1972 at the Shubert Theater,"
        Facts on File Yearbook, 1972, p. 1071 (A1).

1089.   "The Creation: The Play Is Closed on December 16,
        after 20 Performances," New York Times, Decem-
        ber 8, 1972, p. 37:2; December 17, 1972, II, 5:6.

1090.   Crowther, Bosley.   "All My Sons," New York Times,
        March 29, 1948, p. 17:3 (FR).

1091.   _____. "Death of a Salesman with Frederic
        March and Mildred Dunnock at Victoria," New York
        Times, December 21, 1951, p. 21:3 (FR).

1092.   _____. "The Misfits," New York Times, Febru-
        ary 2, 1961, p. 24:2 (FR).

1093.   _____. "A View from the Bridge," New York
        Times, January 23, 1962, p. 30:1 (FR).

1094.   _____. "Witches of Salem," New York Times,
        December 19, 1958, p. 54:2 (The Crucible) (FR).

1095.   "The Crucible: A Review," Times (London), May 13,
        1972, p. 10c.

1096.   "The Crucible Opens at the Lincoln Center on April
        28, 1972," Facts on File Yearbook, 1972, p. 474
        (F2).

1097.   "Cultural Freedom Committee Denies Asking State-
        ment; M's Reply," New York Times, February 14,
        1956, p. 5:1.

1098.   "Curbs on Americans: House, 373-9, Cites M for
        Contempt," New York Times, July 26, 1956, p. 7:1.

1099.   Darlington, W. A. "London Sees M's Death of a
        Salesman," New York Times, August 7, 1949, II, 4-
        7 (R).

1100.   "A Daughter, Born to M and His Wife, the Former
        Ingeborg Morath, on September 15, 1962 (Rebecca
        Augusta)," New York Times, September 29, 1962, p.
        15:3.

1101.   "Death of a Salesman," Christian Science Monitor,
        March 5, 1949, p. 12 (R).

1102.   "Death of a Salesman Acclaimed in Vienna," New
        York Times, March 4, 1950, p. 10.

1103.   "Death of a Salesman: Comment on Musical Accom-
        paniment," New York Times, March 27, 1949, II,
        1:2.

1104.   "Death of a Salesman (Copenhagen)," New York Times,
        March 16, 1950, p. 41:4.

1105.   "Death of a Salesman: Film Made of AM's Play with-
        out His Knowledge: M and Columbia Pictures to
        Check Copyright Infringement of 1951 Film," New
        York Times, March 10, 1961, p. 24:3.

1106.   "Death of a Salesman: F. Kortner to Offer Play,
        Berlin," New York Times, June 9, 1949, p. 35:1.

1107.   "Death of a Salesman: Gene Lockhart Replaces L. J.
        Cobb as New Willy Loman," New York Times, Novem-
        ber 10, 1949, p. 40:2 (R).

1108.   "Death of a Salesman: Glenwood Landing, N. Y.,
        Troupe Decides to Produce Play despite Leading Man
        T. E. Paradine Walkout to Protest Author's Alleged
        Left-Wing Affiliations," New York Times, November
        12, 1954, p. 23:3.

1109.   "Death of a Salesman in Denmark: M's Play Is Laud-
        ed by Copenhagen Critics," New York Times, March
        16, 1950, p. 41 (R).

1110.   "Death of a Salesman: M Gets New York Newspaper
        Guild Page One Award," New York Times, March 29,
        1949, p. 21:7.

1111. "Death of a Salesman: M Gets Jewish Writers, Artists, and Scientists American Committee Award,"
New York Times, June 1, 1949, p. 43:2.

1112. "Death of a Salesman: Moves Londoner," New York
Times, July 29, 1949, p. 12:5 (R).

1113. "Death of a Salesman (Munich and Dusseldorf, Germany)," New York Times, April 28, 1950, p. 25:4
(R).

1114. "Death of a Salesman: New York Drama Critics'
Circle Award Presented," New York Times, April 17,
1949, p. 63:6.

1115. "Death of a Salesman Opens," New York Times, August 14, 1954, p. 8:4.

1116. "Death of a Salesman Opens in Two German Cities:
Munich and Dusseldorf," New York Times, April 28,
1950, p. 25.

1117. "Death of a Salesman: To Close on Jan. 28, Because
of P. Muni's Ill Health (London)," New York Times,
December 11, 1949, p. 84:6.

1118. "Death of a Salesman (Vienna)," New York Times,
March 4, 1950, p. 10:7.

1119. "Death of a Salesman Wins American Theatre Wing
Award," New York Times, April 25, 1949, p. 17:3.

1120. "Death of a Salesman: Wins Billboard's Donaldson
Award," New York Times, July 1949, XII, 31:1.

1121. "Death of a Salesman Wins New York Drama Critics'
Circle Award," New York Times, April 13, 1949, p.
40:4.

1122. "Death of a Salesman Wins Pulitzer Prize," New York
Times, May 3, 1949, p. 1:6; May 3, 1949, p. 22:1,
p. 24:3; Comments on Awards, May 15, 1949, II, 1:1.

1123. "Death of a Salesman Wins Theatre Club Award,"
New York Times, April 4, 1949, p. 26:1.

1124. Dedmon, Emmett. "Death of a Salesman," Chicago

Sun, May 22, 1949, p. 8 x (R).

1125. Dekker, Albert. "Death of a Salesman: Albert Dek-
      ker Article of Understanding Role for New York and
      Chicago Productions," New York Times, April 30,
      1950, II, 2:6-8.

1126. "Denied Passport by State Department to Visit Brus-
      sels to Open His Play," New York Times, March 31,
      1954, p. 16:3.

1127. "DeWitt Clinton: Teachers Union Urges Dr. Walsh
      and Assistant Superintendent Ernst to Lift Ban on L.
      Z. Hobson and AM Books," New York Times, Febru-
      ary 16, 1948, p. 23:7.

1128. "Divorce from M. Monroe Granted, Property Settle-
      ment Made," New York Times, January 25, 1961, p.
      35:4.

1129. "Divorced from His Wife, the Former Mary Grace
      Slattery," New York Times, June 12, 1956, p. 24:6.

1130. Dorn, N. K. "Collected Plays," San Francisco
      Chronicle, June 2, 1957, p. 24 (R).

1131. Dorn, N.K. "Collected Plays," Kirkus, 25 (March
      15, 1957), 256 (R).

1132. "Drama by AM Opens in London," New York Times,
      October 12, 1956, p. 35:3 (A View from the Bridge)
      (R).

1133. Duffield, Maurice. "Situation Normal," Kirkus, 12
      (September 15, 1944), 419 (R).

1134. "E. German Newspaper Reports French-E. German
      Companies Plan Film on M's The Crucible," New
      York Times, July 9, 1956, p. 3:6.

1135. Eaton, W. P. "Death of a Salesman," New York
      Herald Tribune, May 22, 1949, p. 6 (R).

1136. "Elected to National Arts and Letters Institute," New
      York Times, February 11, 1958, p. 28:3.

1137. "An Enemy of the People Produced March 11, 1971,

at the Vivian Beaumont Theater at Lincoln Center,"
Facts on File, 1971.

1138.   "Estimate Board Evades Decision on Contract with
        Combined Artists for Film on Youth Board Activities
        as Corp. Counsel Brown Rules Youth Board Can Make
        Own Decision," New York Times, November 30, 1955,
        p. 38:7.

1139.   "Executive Committee Nominates M (US) for Interna-
        tional President of the PEN," New York Times, May
        23, 1965, VII, 8.

1140.   "Ex-Senator Cain Testifies He Believes M Was Never
        Under Communist Discipline," New York Times, May
        24, 1957, p. 9:2.

1141.   "Facsimile of Marilyn Monroe in M's Play," Times,
        January 24, 1964, p. 8 (After the Fall).

1142.   Farrell, Isolde. "Les Sorcieres de Salem," New
        York Times, February 27, 1955, II, 3:1 (The Cruci-
        ble) (R).

1143.   "Fellowship of Reconciliation Sponsors 'Poets for
        Peace' Reading, New York City," New York Times,
        November 13, 1967, p. 60:3.

1144.   "5th Dartmouth Conf. Ends, Attended by AM," New
        York Times, January 21, 1969, p. 3:4.

1145.   "Focus," New York Herald Tribune Books. Novem-
        ber 18, 1945, p. 4 (R).

1146.   "Found in Contempt of Congress," New York Times,
        June 1, 1957, p. 1:1.

1147.   Frank, Stanley. "AM, Whose Death of a Salesman
        Has Started a Trend, Comes Up with Provocative
        Ideas about the Medium," TV Guide, 14 (October 8,
        1966), 6-11.

1148.   Freedley, George. "The Crucible," Kirkus, 21
        (March 15, 1953), 207 (R).

1149.   _____. "Death of a Salesman," Kirkus, 17 (March
        1, 1949), 125 (R).

1150. "French Company Denies East German Link in Pro-
       ducing M's The Crucible," New York Times, July 10,
       1956, p. 26:5.

1151. Funke, Lewis. "M's Drama Revived at New Theatre,"
       New York Times, March 12, 1958, p. 36:1 (The
       Crucible) (R).

1152. "Gasoline Rations Suspended," New York Times, June
       2, 1944, p. 17:5.

1153. "Gets His Honorary Degree, University of Michigan,"
       New York Times, June 17, 1956, p. 8:1.

1154. "Gets New York Drama Critics' Circle Award," New
       York Times, April 22, 1947, p. 33:3.

1155. Gilman, Richard. "After the Fall," Chicago Sun
       Book Week, March 8, 1964, p. 6 (R).

1156. Gould, Jack. "AM's High Pitched The Crucible (TV),"
       New York Times, May 5, 1967, p. 79:1 (R).

1157. _____. "AM's Play, The Price," New York Times,
       February 4, 1971, p. 71:3 (R).

1158. Greenfield, Joseph. "Writing Plays Is Absolutely
       Senseless, AM Says, 'But I Love It. I Just Love It',"
       New York Times Magazine, pp. 16-17, 34-39, [The
       Creation of the World and Other Business, etc.].
       See also entry 399.

1159. [No entry.]

1160. Gussow, Mel. "Death of a Salesman Presented Cen-
       ter Stage, Baltimore with an All-Black Cast," New
       York Times, April 9, 1972, p. 69:1 (R).

1161. _____. "Stage: Black 'Salesman': Baltimore
       Production of Play by M Shows Willy's Value to Be
       White," New York Times, April 9, 1972, p. 69:1
       [Death of a Salesman] (R).

1162. "H. Breit Comment on Views of M and Farrell,"
       New York Times, February 26, 1956, VII, 8:2.

1163. Hawkins, William. "Death of a Salesman: Powerful

Tragedy," New York-World Telegram, February 11, 1949, p. 16; AM, "Death of a Salesman": Text and Criticism, ed. Gerald Weales, pp. 202-04.

1164. "Hebrew Union in Jerusalem ... AM to Be Honored By American Friends," New York Times, September 9, 1959, p. 50:5.

1165. "His Mother Dies of a Heart Ailment at 70 (Mrs. Augusta M, the wife of Isadore M, a Salesman)," New York Times, March 7, 1961, p. 35:3.

1166. Hobson, Harold. "Fair Play," Sunday Times (London), November 14, 1954, p. 11; AM, "The Crucible": Text and Criticism, ed. Gerald Weales, pp. 227-30.

1167. Hogan, William. "The Crucible," New York Herald Tribune Book Review, June 7, 1953, p. 6 (R).

1168. "Hollywood Production," New York Times, March 17, 1958, p. 21:1 (The Crucible).

1169. "House Un-American Activities Committee Votes Contempt Citation for M," New York Times, July 11, 1956, p. 10:5.

1170. Huston, Luther A. "M's Past Tie with Reds Retold; Author's Counsel Overruled on Protest of Irrelevancy at Contempt Trial," New York Times, May 16, 1957, p. 17:3.

1171. Hutchens, John K. "The Misfits," New York Herald Tribune Lively Arts, February 5, 1961, p. 27 (R).

1172. _____. "Mr. M Has a Change of Luck," New York Times, February 23, 1947, II, 1 & 3.

1173. "I Don't Need You Any More," Times Literary Supplement, November 30, 1967, p. 1125.

1174. "I Don't Need You Any More, Collection of Short Stories," New York Times, March 18, 1967, p. 27:1; April 2, 1967, VII, 1 (R).

1175. "Illustrated," New York Times, May 15, 1957, p. 19:4; July 20, 1957, p. 4:3.

1176. "In Brighton, England, M Hospitalized with Hepatitis," New York Times, January 20, 1966, p. 19:2.

1177. "In Moscow with Wife," New York Times, February 3, 1965, p. 30:4.

1178. "In New York City; Illustrated," New York Times, August 28, 1956, p. 13:2.

1179. "In New York City with M. Monroe," New York Times, November 22, 1956, p. 50:8.

1180. "In Paris," New York Times, February 8, 1964, p. 15:2.

1181. "In Russia with Inge Morath," Times Literary Supplement, January 22, 1970, p. 76 (R).

1182. "Incident at Vichy: Author Reads Play to Lincoln Center Repertory Company," New York Times, August 27, 1964, p. 28:1.

1183. "Incident at Vichy in London Premiere," New York Times, Jan. 27, 1966, p. 28:5 (R).

1184. "Incident at Vichy: Letters on Earlier Review," New York Times, December 20, 1964, II, 7:1.

1185. "Incident at Vichy: M Expected to Withdraw Play from Lincoln Center in Wake of Center Dispute," New York Times, January 1, 1965, X:3.

1186. "Inquiry Reform Seen Inevitable Congress Mulls Implications of Watkins Case: AM Asks Reversal," New York Times, June 19, 1957, p. 16:2.

1187. "It Happened in Vichy and After the Fall in Russia," Akron Beacon Journal, March 16, 1967.

1188. "Izvestia Article Scores Participation in Conference by A. J. Goldberg, AM, and Senators A. A. Ribicoff and J. K. Javits," New York Times, February 20, 1971, p. 1:2.

1189. "Judge Kaplan Says ACLU Is Only Organ That Approved Plan; Says Commissioner Tenney Report Showed M's Former Ties to Subversive Groups," New York

Times, December 8, 1955, p. 47:7.

1190. "Judge McLaughlin Refuses to Strike from Record
      Government Testimony Designed to Show M Was Com-
      munist in Mid-40s," New York Times, May 21, 1957,
      p. 30:7; April 13, 1957, p. 9:4; May 4, 1957, p.
      26:7.

1191. Kennedy, Leo. "Focus," Chicago Sun Book Week,
      November 11, 1945, p. 28 (R).

1192. Kerr, Walter F. "AM, Stuck with the Book: 'The
      Creation'," New York Times, December 10, 1972,
      II, 3 and 5 (R).

1193. _____. "The Creation of the World and Other
      Business," New York Times, December 10, 1972,
      II, 5:6 (R).

1194. _____. "The Crucible," New York Herald Tribune,
      January 23, 1953, p. 12; AM, "The Crucible": Text
      and Criticism, ed. Gerald Weales, pp. 189-91.

1195. _____. "The Crucible," New York Times, May
      7, 1972, II, 3:1 (R).

1196. _____. "Mr. M's Two New Faces: The Price,"
      New York Times, February 18, 1968, II, 1:1 (R).

1197. "King Bros. Buy Film Right to Book, Focus," New
      York Times, July 21, 1946, II, 3:6.

1198. Krutch, Joseph Wood. "Death of a Salesman,"
      Manchester Guardian, August 23, 1949, p. 3 (R).

1199. _____. "Ten American Plays That Will Endure,"
      New York Times Magazine, October 11, 1959, pp.
      34-35, 69-70 (Death of a Salesman).

1200. Kupferberg, Herbert. "Situation Normal," New York
      Herald Tribune, December 17, 1944, p. 8 (R).

1200a. "L. Tyrmand Letter Rebuts Tyron and M Defense of
       Yevtushenko," New York Times, December 8, 1968,
       VI, 13:2.

1201. Lask, Thomas. "I Don't Need You Any More," New

York Times, March 18, 1967, p. 27 (R).

1202. _____. "A Memory of Two Mondays," New York Times, January 29, 1971, p. 9:1 (R).

1203. Lenoir, Jean-Piere. "Paris Critics Cold to After the Fall," New York Times, January 25, 1965, p. 21:6 (R).

1204. Leonard, William. "The Misfits," Chicago Sun Tribune, February 12, 1961, p. 6 (R).

1205. "Letter," New York Times, May 17, 1953, II, 3:8.

1206. "Letter by AM Is Read at Committee for a Free Press Meeting," New York Times, February 14, 1972, p. 26:3.

1207. "Letter in Support of Solzhenitsyn Signed by AM, Aug. 14, 1968," Facts on File, 1968.

1208. "Letter on Dismissal of Jewish Dancer V. Panov from Kirov State Dance Theatre; Signed by AM," New York Times, June 19, 1972, p. 32:5.

1209. "Letter on M Case Cites Impact Abroad," New York Times, August 8, 1956, p. 24:6.

1210. "Letter Urges M Be Judged by His Script," New York Times, December 15, 1955, p. 36:6.

1211. "Letters," New York Times, February 15, 1953, II, 3:7.

1212. "Letters about M's Letter on Authors' Lacking Originality," New York Times, August 17, 1952, II, 1:4.

1213. "Letters by Members of NYC Theatre Community Denounce as Cultural Repression Reported Arrest of Brazilian Theatre Director A. Boal," New York Times, April 24, 1971, p. 28:5.

1214. "Letters on NYT Survey of Future of Broadway," New York Times, January 11, 1970, II, 6:5.

1215. "Letters on Novick Review of A Memory of Two Mondays," New York Times, February 28, 1971, II, 17:7.

1216. "Letters on The Price," New York Times, May 12, 1968, II, 51.

1217. Lewis, Anthony. "A Red Party Link to M: Application Card Produced by House Unit; Playwright Says He Had No Part in It," New York Times, August 25, 1957, p. 20:1.

1218. "Lincoln Center, New York City: Repertory Theater Dispute, Spurred by Broadway's Attempt to Hire Opera Executives and Causing Resignation of R. Whitehead, E. Kazan, and AM from Theater Posts, Results in M's Withdrawal of His Two Plays (After the Fall and Incident at Vichy) in June and Cancellation of Theater's 4th Play, The Madwoman of Chaillot," New York Times, January 1, 1965, X: 10:3; January 24, 1965, p. 82:4; October 26, 1962, p. 25:1.

1219. Loftus, Joseph A. "AM and Dr. Nathan Indicted on Contempt Charges," New York Times, February 19, 1957, p. 1:5.

1220. "London Critics Call Drama 'Best Serious' Play from America," New York Times, May 12, 1948, p. 33:3 (All My Sons) (R).

1221. "London Critics Hail M's The Crucible," New York Times, April 11, 1956, p. 28:3.

1222. [No entry.]

1223. "McCarthy Candidates for Delegates Include Prof. J. Tobin, AM, W. Styron, C. Kerr, Mrs. L. H. Pollack," New York Times, March 10, 1968, p. 48:1.

1224. McLaughlin, Richard. "The Misfits," Springfield Republican, March 12, 1961, p. 5 (R).

1225. Maloney, Russell. "Situation Normal," New York Times, December 24, 1944, p. 3 (R).

1226. "Marilyn Monroe Seeks Mexican Divorce," New York Times, January 22, 1961, p. 86:2.

1227. "M, ACLU Score Board Move," New York Times, December 9, 1955, p. 29:4.

1228. "M, Affidavit Denying Ever under Communist Discipline Placed in Record," New York Times, May 17, 1957, p. 10:4.

1229. "M Again President," New York Times, August 1, 1967, p. 33:1.

1230. "M and Monroe Leave for London on Honeymoon-Business Trip," New York Times, July 14, 1956, p. 33:2.

1231. "M and Nathan Disavow Contempt," New York Times, March 2, 1957, p. 14:2.

1232. "M Appeals," New York Times, June 12, 1958, p. 26:5.

1233. "M Asks Reversal; New Appeal Urges Acquittal without Formalities," New York Times, July 26, 1957, p. 8:3.

1234. "M Buys Home, Brooklyn," New York Times, June 1, 1947, VIII, 1:7.

1235. "M Comments on Reaction Abroad to His Plays," New York Times, July 21, 1957, II, 1:1.

1236. "M Denounces Political Interference with Art," New York Times, February 13, 1956, p. 9:2.

1237. "M Donates Mss. and Other Papers to University of Texas Humanities Research Center," New York Times, February 13, 1962, p. 38:1.

1238. "M Feted by Viking Press to Mark Sale of One Millionth Paperback Edition of Death of a Salesman," New York Times, March 8, 1968, p. 36:1.

1239. "M Files Appeal, Links Conviction to Romance with Marilyn Monroe," New York Times, February 22, 1958, p. 6:2.

1240. "M Holds Department of State Interferes with Circulation of American Arts Abroad," New York Times, May 7, 1957, p. 5:3.

1241. "M Is Working on New Play," New York Times, June 25, 1971, p. 16:1; February 7, 1971, II, 1:2; Illus.,

February 7, 1971, II, 17:1.

1242. "M Refuses to Give House Un-American Activities Committee Names of Those Who Attended Communist Writers Meeting, 1939 or 1940; Walter Hints Contempt Citation," New York Times, July 8, 1956, p. 25:1.

1243. "M Rejects White House Invitation to Bill-Signing Ceremony Because of Disagreement with Adam's Vietnam Policy," New York Times, September 28, 1965, II, p. 4; New York Times, February 13, 1965, p. 9:2.

1244. "M Responds to Criticism That Play (The Price) Is Divorced from Current Problems," New York Times, March 5, 1968, p. 32:1.

1245. "M Returns to U.S. After Honeymoon Trip to London," New York Times, August 27, 1956, p. 15:2.

1246. "M Scores USSR Censorship of F. M. Dostoevski, Others, Statement Marking Anniversary of Dostoevski's Death," New York Times, February 13, 1956, p. 2.

1247. "M Trial Opens: His Attorney Rauh Holds Questions M Refused to Answer in 1956 Were Not Pertinent; Denies M Was Ever Communist Party Member," New York Times, May 15, 1957, p. 19:4

1248. "M's After the Fall Seen at Paris American Church," New York Times, February 1, 1966, p. 26:1 (R).

1249. "M's Article Charges Authors Lack Originality," New York Times, August 10, 1952, II, 1:1.

1250. "M's Article Criticizes Casting Method," New York Times, August 21, 1955, II, 1:1, 5.

1251. "M's Efforts to Get Funds for Showing His Play, All My Sons, at Prague Youth Festival, Fail," New York Times, June 11, 1947, p. 33:2; "Comment," June 12, 1947, p. 24:4.

1252. "M's Letter Queries Propriety of Presenting Classic Works on TV," New York Times, November 29, 1959, II. 13:1.

1253. "M's Reaction to Opening Nights of His Own Plays
Discussed," New York Times, December 12, 1954,
VI, 12.

1254. "M's The Price Acclaimed by Critics in London,"
New York Times, March 6, 1969, p. 36:2 (R).

1255. "M's Work Hailed: A View from the Bridge Wins
Ovation on Cape Cod," New York Times, August 31,
1955, p. 16:8.

1256. Millstein, Gilbert. "Ten Playwrights Tell How It All
Starts," New York Times Magazine, December 6,
1959, pp. 63-65.

1257. "The Misfits," Times (London) Literary Supplement,
May 12, 1961, p. 296 (R).

1258. "Mrs. L. B. Johnson in Lincoln Center to See M's
Play," New York Times, December 7, 1964, p. 16:
27.

1259. Mitgang, Herbert. "The Misfits," New York Times,
February 8, 1961, p. 29:3 (R).

1260. "Moscow Radio Sympathizes with M: Links His Play,
The Crucible and Incident at Vichy," New York Times,
February 20, 1957, p. 2:5.

1261. "National Institute of Arts and Letters Annual Cere-
monies Described by AM as Attempt to Afford People
in Arts Opportunity to Communicate," New York
Times, May 18, 1972, p. 49:1.

1262. "National Repertory Theater," New York Times, April 7, 1964, p. 30:2 (The Crucible).

1263. "National Theater, London, Staged by Sir Laurence
Olivier," New York Times, January 20, 1965, p. 35:
1 (The Crucible).

1264. "NBC on June 26 Announces Its Schedule of TV Spe-
cials, M's Play After the Fall Will be First Special,"
New York Times, June 27, 1973, p. 111:1.

1265. "New Plea by M, Acquittal Urged on Basis of Court

Action in Singer Case," New York Times, July 17,
1957, p. 3:3.

1266. New York Times, March 31, 1954, p. 16; October 26,
1955, pp. 1, 62; November 30, 1955, p. 38; December 8, 1955, p. 33; June 22, 1956, p. 1; February
19, 1957, p. 1; June 1, 1957, p. 1; July 20, 1957, p.
4. (Key news reports on M's troubles with the State
Department, the New York City Youth Board, and the
House Committee on Un-American Activities).

1267. "New York World's Fair, 1964: AM, Heckscher and
Other Top Leaders in the Arts Deplore Absence of
Pavilion for Contemporary Art," New York Times,
November 18, 1963, p. 35:1 & 2.

1268. Nichols, Lewis. "The Man Who Had All the Luck,"
New York Times, November 24, 1944, p. 18:5 (R).

1269. Novick, J. "A Memory of Two Mondays," New York
Times, February 7, 1971, p. 17:7 (R).

1270. _____. "The Price," New York Times, Feb. 7,
1971, II, 17:7 (R).

1271. "Orders Probe of Charges That Film Script Writer,
Playwright M, Has Left-Wing Ties," New York Times,
October 25, 1955, p. 1:5.

1272. "Our Colossal Dad," Times (London) Literary Supplement, August 1958, p. 482 (AM's Collected Plays);
also in Two Modern American Tragedies, ed. John
D. Hurrell. New York: Scribner's, 1961, pp. 72-
75 (R).

1273. "P. Emmanuel (France) Succeeds AM as President of
PEN," New York Times, September 16, 1969, p. 43:1.

1274. Peck, Seymour. "Growth--and Growing Pains--of an
Actor: Arthur Kennedy's Role," New York Times
Magazine, February 15, 1953, VI, 20, 34, 36.

1275. "PEN President Miller Says Writers Are Gaining in
Influence and in Political and Social Power," New
York Times, July 6, 1965, p. 30:5.

1276. Peterson, Ralph. "Situation Normal," Chicago Sun

Book Week, December 17, 1944, p. 3 (R).

1277. Phelan, Kappo. "Death of a Salesman," Cleveland Open Shelf, July 1949, p. 14 (R).

1278. "Phoenix Theatre in New York City: T. Guthrie, AM Speak," New York Times, April 29, 1959, p. 28:4.

1279. "Plays to Be Published in USSR," New York Times, August 11, 1960, p. 6:3.

1280. "Playwright L. Hellman Letter on T. Buckley Article on AM Play," New York Times, January 21, 1973, II, 18:2 (The Creation of the World and Other Business).

1281. "The Price," Times (London) Literary Supplement, October 10, 1968, p. 1154 (R).

1282. "The Price Closes on B'Way; AM Works with Cast to Prepare for London Production," New York Times, March 6, 1969, p. 36:2.

1283. "The Price Produced. Feb. 7, 1968, at Morosco Theater," Facts in File, 1968.

1284. "The Price to Close After 425 Performances," New York Times, January 14, 1969, p. 36:2.

1285. "Proceedings Against M: A Report from Committee on Un-American Activities Citing M, July 25, 1956, p. 38 [House Reports on Public Bills. 84th Congress. 14963-2922]," Monthly Catalog (September 1956), p. 39.

1286. "Prof. P. E. Sigmund Letter on AM Sept. 15 Article," New York Times, October 13, 1968, VI, 32.

1287. "Prof. Sidorsky Disputes AM Article," New York Times, December 26, 1970, p. 16:3.

1288. "Protested Play Given: Glen Players Open Death of a Salesman with New Lead (in Long Island)," New York Times, December 10, 1954, p. 42.

1289. "Pulitzer Prizes Announced: M," New York Times, May 3, 1949, p. 1:6.

1290. Raymont, Henry. "U.S. Bars Cubans from Film
       Event: Refusal of Visas on Political Bias Stirs Pro-
       tests [from AM & Others]," New York Times, March
       24, 1972, p. 8:1.

1291. Reeve, F. D. "In Russia with Inge Morath," Book
       World, January 4, 1970, p. 11 (R).

1292. "Rejects Hollywood Writing Offer," New York Times,
       July 17, 1947, p. 15:1.

1293. "Reported July 18, 1968, that Xuan Thuy had singled
       out the alliance for special comment at a meeting in
       Paris with American playwright AM and other oppo-
       nents of U.S. policy in Vietnam," Facts on File,
       1968.

1294. "Retiring PEN President AM Urges Young Writers
       Take Active Role in World," New York Times, Sep-
       tember 19, 1969, p. 43:1.

1295. "Review of the 500th Performance," New York Times,
       May 17, 1959; II, 1:6; May 27, 1959, p. 30:2; June
       16, 1959, p. 39:2.

1296. "Revised Bridge Given in Capital Arena Stage Offers
       M's Waterfront Drama in New Hospitality Home," New
       York Times, November 9, 1956, p. 34:4.

1297. "Reweds in Jewish Faith (M. Monroe)," New York
       Times, July 3, 1956, p. 16:2.

1298. Ross, J. L. "Focus," Kirkus, 13 (August 15, 1945),
       345 (R).

1299. Rossellini, R. "Squardo dal Ponte, Based on M's A
       View from the Bridge World Premiere, Rome," New
       York Times, March 13, 1961, p. 36:5.

1300. Rosten, N. "A View from the Bridge," New York
       Times, January 21, 1962, II, 9:3 (FR).

1301. "Roxburg Public Library: M. Lee, W. C. Styron, J.
       H. Humphrey Elected Directors; AM Defeated," New
       York Times, October 6, 1963, p. 37:4.

1302. "S. Jacobson Letter," New York Times, April 25,

1954, II, 3:8.

1303. Salisbury, Harrison E.   "In Russia with Inge Morath,"
       New York Times Book Review, December 14, 1969,
       p. 1 (R).

1304. "Saw Warsaw University," New York Times, Febru-
       ary 17, 1965, p. 35:4.

1305. "Situation Normal," New York Herald Tribune Books,
       December 17, 1944, p. 8 (R).

1306. "State Department Grants 6-Month Passport," New
       York Times, July 7, 1956, p. 15:7.

1307. "State Department Refuses Visas to 4 Cuban Film Di-
       rectors; Critics Include AM," New York Times,
       March 24, 1972, p. 8:1.

1308. Szogy, Alex.   "Harold Clurman's On Directing; Illus-
       tration of Clurman with AM, Director," New York
       Times Book Review, November 19, 1972, p. 28.

1309. "T. Buckley Article on Problems Encountered in Pro-
       duction of The Creation of the World and Other Busi-
       ness," New York Times, December 5, 1972, p. 49:1.

1310. Taubman, Howard.   "After the Fall," New York
       Times, February 2, 1964, II, 1:1 (R).

1311. _____.   "AM Drama at Belasco Theatre," New
       York Times, April 7, 1964, p. 30:2 (The Crucible)
       (R).

1312. _____.   "AM's After the Fall," New York Times,
       February 2, 1964, II, 1.

1313. _____.   "AM's Play After the Fall," New York
       Times, January 24, 1964, p. 18.

1314. _____.   "AM's Play Opens Repertory," New York
       Times, January 24, 1964, p. 18:1 (After the Fall)
       (R).

1315. _____.   "Death of a Salesman," New York Times,
       March 27, 1949, II, 1:2 (R).

1316.   _____. "Death of a Salesman Done in Minnesota,"
New York Times, July 20, 1963, p. 11:2 (R).

1317.   _____. "Incident at Vichy," New York Times, December 4, 1964, p. 30:2 (R).

1318.   _____. "Incident at Vichy," New York Times, December 20, 1964, II, 3 (R).

1319.   _____. "Inquiry into Roots of Evil: Incident at
Vichy," New York Times, December 20, 1964, II, 3:
1 (R).

1320.   _____. "The Price in Tel Aviv," New York Times,
October 19, 1968, II, 1:1 (R).

1321.   _____. "Tel Aviv Hebrew Language Production of
The Price," New York Times, October 19, 1968, p.
29:1 (R).

1322.   _____. "Theater: M Revival: A View from the
Bridge at Sheridan Square," New York Times, January 29, 1965, p. 24:1 (R).

1323.   "$10-Gala for McCarthy at Cheetah Described," New
York Times, August 15, 1973, p. 34:4.

1324.   Torry, C, V, "All My Sons," New York Herald Tribune Weekly Book Review, March 0, 1947, p 19 (R).

1325.   _____. "All My Sons," New York Times, April
6, 1947, p. 12 (R).

1326.   "Theatre Director H. Clurman's Book, On Directing
Reviewed by A. Szogy; Illus. of Clurman with AM,"
New York Times, November 19, 1972, VII, 28.

1327.   Thompson, Howard. "After the Fall Bought for Film;
M Sells Screen Rights for Reported $500,000," New
York Times, June 27, 1964, p. 14.

1328.   "To Wed M. Monroe," New York Times, June 22,
1956, p. 1:3.

1329.   "22 American Writers Urge Soviet Writers to Use
Their Influence in Restoring Jewish Cultural Interests,"
New York Times, May 21, 1967, p. 12:1.

1330. "Two Articles to Debate Play (The Price)," New
       York Times, April 14, 1968, II, 1:7; reply, April 21,
       1968, II, 1:4.

1331. "United Aircraft Corp. on Nov. 15 Files $1-million
       Suit Charging H. Harrington, Jr., and AM," New
       York Times, November 16, 1972, p. 74:8.

1332. "U.S. Appeals Court Agrees to Hear AM Appeal,"
       New York Times, May 28, 1958, p. 21:6.

1333. "U.S. Appeals Court Reverses M Contempt of Con-
       gress Conviction; M Hails Decision," New York Times,
       August 8, 1958, p. 1:4.

1334. "U.S.: B. Atkinson Cites M's View on Issues in
       Harper's Article," New York Times, November 11,
       1960, p. 28:5.

1335. "USSR Removes from Theatre Repertoire All AM
       Plays," New York Times, November 24, 1970, p. 3:5.

1336. "Various Writers and Artists Have Contributed Works
       to Fund-Raising Auction for Fellowship of Reconcilia-
       tion," New York Times, May 31, 1972, p. 37:2.

1337. "A View from the Bridge," Spectator, 197 (October
       19, 1956), 538+ (R).

1338. "A View from the Bridge: A Child in Audience
       Kicks Actor F. Silvera during Performance, Holly-
       wood: Silvera, in Hospital, Comments," New York
       Times, October 30, 1958, p. 36:1.

1339. "A View from the Bridge, an Opera by R. Rossellini,
       Based on AM's Play: U.S. Premiere Set," New York
       Times, October 15, 1967, II, 19:6; "Performance,"
       October 19, 1967, p. 56:1.

1340. "A View from the Bridge Is Greeted Warmly at New
       Comedy Theatre Club," New York Times, October 12,
       1956, p. 35.

1341. "A View from the Bridge: Reaction, Comedy, The-
       atre, London; Play Presented at Private Club Because
       of Lord Chamberlain's Ban," New York Times, Oc-
       tober 12, 1956, p. 35:3.

1342. "A View from the Bridge: Revised Version, Arena
Stage Production, Washington, D.C.," New York
Times, November 9, 1956, p. 34:4.

1343. "Wagner Admits He Ordered Investigation Committee
Probe of M; He Says He Did Not See Reports, Which
Show No Evidence of M's Leftist Ties Now," New
York Times, November 30, 1955, p. 38:7.

1344. Wain, John. "Literature and Life--I: AM," Observer, September 8, 1957, p. 5.

1345. Wakeman, John. "I Don't Need You Any More," New
York Times, April 2, 1967, p. 4 (R).

1346. Watt, Douglas. "Incident at Vichy," New York Daily
News, December 4, 1964, p. 64 (R).

1347. "Weds I. Morath," New York Times, February 22,
1962, p. 19:3.

1348. "Weds M. Monroe," New York Times, June 30, 1956,
p. 19:3.

1349. Wertham, Frederic. "Death of a Salesman," New
York Herald Tribune Weekly Book Review, May 22,
1949, p. 6 (R).

1350. _____. "Let the Salesman Beware," Now York
Times Book Review, May 15, 1949, pp. 4 & 12
(Death of a Salesman) (R).

1351. "W. German Playwright R. Hochhuth Open Letter
Urges Ban on Works of A. Solzhenitsyn, AM Also
Signed," New York Times, August 15, 1968, p. 14:7.

1352. "Western Intellectuals (Including AM) Send Letters to
Moscow Condemning Solzhenitsyn's Expulsion," New
York Times, December 5, 1969, p. 47:5.

1353. White, W. R. "Death of a Salesman," San Francisco
Chronicle, May 22, 1949, p. 19 (R).

1354. "Wife M. Monroe Plans Divorce," New York Times,
November 12, 1960, p. 1:1.

1355. "Wins Emmy, June 4, 1967--for Dramatic Writing--

Single program--Death of a Salesman," Facts on File, 1967.

1356. "Witchcraft and Stagecraft," New York Post, February 1, 1953, p. 9 M; AM, "The Crucible": Text and Criticism, ed. Gerald Weales, pp. 197-200.

1357. "Witches of Salem (The Crucible)," Spectator, 199 (September 6, 1957), 310 (FR).

1358. " 'Writers Manifesto' Signed by Over 300 Czech Intellectuals," New York Times, September 4, 1967, p. 1:4.

1359. Young, B. A. "The Crucible Staged by Olivier, Scores in London Opening," New York Times, January 20, 1965, p. 35:1 (R).

1360. "Youth Board Seeks to Avoid Link to Controversy Over M Loyalty," New York Times, December 8, 1955, p. 47:7.

1361. "Youth Board Set to Ratify Pact with Combined Artists for Film Based on M Script," New York Times, December 5, 1955, p. 33:4.

8. BIBLIOGRAPHY

1362. Clurman, Harold, ed. The Portable AM. New York: Viking Press, 1972. "Bibliography," pp. 563-66.

1363. Corrigan, Robert W., ed. AM: A Collection of Critical Essays. Englewood Cliffs, N.J.: Prentice-Hall, 1969. "Selected Bibliography," pp. 173-76.

1364. Eissenstat, Martha Turnquist. "AM: A Bibliography," Modern Drama, 5 (May 1962), 93-106.

1365. Evans, Richard I. Psychology and AM. New York: Dutton, 1969. "Recommended Reading," pp. 129-30.

1366. Hayashi, Tetsumaro. AM Criticism (1930-1967). Metuchen, N.J.: Scarecrow Press, 1969.

1367. _____. "AM: The Dimension of His Art and a Checklist of His Published Works," Serif, 4 (June 1967), 26-32.

1368. Hayman, Ronald. AM (World Dramatists Series, No. 1). New York: Ungar, 1972. "Bibliography," pp. 132-33.

1369. Hogan, Robert. AM (University of Minnesota Pamphlets on American Writers, No. 40). Minneapolis: University of Minnesota Press, 1964. "Selected Bibliography," pp. 46-48.

1370. Moss, Leonard. AM (Twayne United Author Series, No. 115). New York: Twayne, 1967. "Selected Bibliography," pp. 135-53.

1371. Murray, Edward. AM, Dramatist. New York: Ungar, 1967. "Bibliography," pp. 183-86.

1372. Nelson, Benjamin. AM: Portrait of A Playwright.

New York: McKay, 1970. "Selected Bibliography,"
pp. 325-29.

1373. Ungar, Harriet. "The Writings of and About AM:
A Checklist 1936-67," Bulletin of the New York Public Library, 74 (March 1970), 107-34.

1374. Weales, Gerald, ed. AM, "The Crucible": Text and
Criticism. New York: Viking Press, 1971. "Bibliography," pp. 477-84.

1375. _____, ed. AM, "Death of a Salesman": Text
and Criticism. New York, 1967. "Bibliography,"
pp. 422-26.

1376. Welland, Dennis. AM. New York: Grove Press,
1961. "Bibliography," pp. 122-24.

PART III
APPENDICES

APPENDIX I

STANDARD REFERENCE GUIDES CONSULTED

Abstracts of English Studies (Champaign, Ill.: National Council of Teachers of English, 1958-).

American Dissertations on the Drama and the Theatre: A Bibliography, ed. Frederick M. Litto (Kent, Ohio: Kent State University Press, 1969), pp. 241-42.

American Drama Criticism, ed. Helen H. Palmer and Jane Anne Dyson (Hamden, Conn.: Shoe String Press, 1967).

American Literary Manuscripts, comp. Joseph Jones, et al. (Austin: University of Texas Press, 1960).

American Literary Scholarship/An Annual, ed. James Woodress (Durham, N.C.: Duke University Press, 1965-).

American Literature (Annual Bibliography), (Durham, N.C.. Duke University Press, 1929-).

Annual Bibliography of English Language and Literature, ed. Marjory Rigby, et al. (Cambridge, England: Modern Humanities Research Association, 1921-).

Bibliographic Index (New York: Wilson, 1938-).

Bibliography of Bibliographies in American Literature by Charles H. Nilon (New York: Bowker, 1970).

Bibliography of the American Theatre Excluding New York City by Carl J. Stratman (Chicago: Loyola University Press, 1965).

A Bibliography of Theatre Arts Publication in English, 1963, ed. Bernard F. Dukore (Washington, D.C.: American Educational Theatre Association, 1965).

123

Biography Index (New York: Wilson, 1947-).

Book Review Digest (New York: Wilson, 1905-).

Book Review Index (Detroit: Gale Research, 1965-).

British Humanities Index (London: The Library Association, 1962).

Canadian Index to Periodicals and Documentary Films (1960-63) (Ottawa: Canadian Library Association, 1960-).

Catalog of Reprints in Series. 21st edition (Metuchen, N.J.: Scarecrow Press, 1972).

Contemporary Authors: A Bio-Bibliographical Guide to Current Authors and Their Works, ed. James M. Ethridge (Detroit: Gale Research, 1963).

Cumulative Book Index (New York: Wilson, 1933-).

Cumulative Dramatic Index 1909-1949 ed. Frederick W. Faxon, et al. 2 vols. (Boston: G. K. Hall, 1965).

Cumulative Magazine Subject Index 1907-1949. 2 vols. (Boston: G. K. Hall, 1964).

Dissertations in American Literature 1891-1966 by James Woodress and Marian Koritz (Durham, N.C.: Duke University Press, 1968).

Education Index (New York: Wilson, 1932-).

Essay and General Literature Index (New York: Wilson, 1934-).

Filmed Books and Plays 1955-1957: Supplement by A. G. S. Enser (London: Grafton, 1958).

A Guide to Critical Reviews: Part I: American Drama, 1909-1969. By James M. Salem. 2nd edition. Metuchen, N.J.: Scarecrow Press, 1973).

A Guide to Play Selection, 2nd ed. by NCTE (New York: Appleton-Century-Crofts, 1958).

A Guide to the Study of the United States of America (Washington, D. C. : Library of Congress, 1960).

An Index to Book Reviews in the Humanities (Detroit: Philip
Thomson, 1960-).

Index to Little Magazines, ed. Dorella Fuhs (Chicago: Swal-
low Press, 1948-).

International Index to Periodicals (see Social Sciences and
Humanities Index).

International Motion Picture Almanac, ed. Charles S. Aaron-
son (New York: Quigley Publications, 1929-).

The Library Journal Book Review (New York: Bowker,
1968-).

A Library of Literary Criticism: Modern American Literature, ed. Dorothy Nyren (New York: Ungar, 1960), pp.
337-41.

Literary and Library Prizes, ed. Jeanne J. Henderson and
Brenda G. Piggins (New York: Bowker, 1973).

MLA International Bibliography (New York: MLA, 1921-).

Modern Drama (Toronto, Ontario, Canada: A. M. Hakkert,
1958-).

Modern Drama: A Checklist of Critical Literature on 20th
Century Plays by Irving Adelman and Rita Dworkin
(Metuchen, N. J. : Scarecrow Press, 1967).

National Union Catalog (New York: Rowman and Littlefield,
1942-).

New York Times Index (New York: New York Times,
1913-).

Play Index 1949-1952, comp. Dorothy Herbert West and
Dorothy Margaret Peake (New York: Wilson, 1953-).

Play Index 1953-1960, comp. Estelle A. Fidell and Dorothy
Margaret Peake (New York: Wilson, 1963).

Play Index 1961-1967, ed. Estelle A. Fidell (New York:
Wilson, 1968).

The Player's Library, the Catalog of the Library of the British Drama League (London: Faber and Faber, 1954,
1956).

Psychoanalysis, Psychology, and Literature: A Bibliography,
comp. Norman Kiell (Madison: University of Wisconsin
Press, 1963).

The Reader's Adviser, rev. Winifred F. Courtney. 11th ed.
(New York: Bowker, 1969).

Readers' Guide to Periodical Literature (New York: Wilson,
1905-).

Short Story Index (New York: Wilson, 1969).

Social Sciences and Humanities Index (formerly International
Index to Periodicals) (New York: Wilson, 1916-).

Subject Guide to Books in Print (New York: Bowker, 1957-).

Theses in American Literature 1896-1971 by Patsy C. Howard (Ann Arbor, Mich.:   Pierian Press, 1973).

A Title Guide to the Talkies (1927-1963) by Richard B. Dim-
mit (Metuchen, N.J.:   Scarecrow Press, 1965).

Whitaker's Cumulative Book List (London: Whitaker, 1924-).

APPENDIX II

A LIST OF NEWSPAPERS, PERIODICALS, AND ANNUALS INDEXED

[For full bibliographical details, consult Ulrich's International Periodicals Directory.]

Akron Beacon Journal
America
American-German Review
American Mercury
American Record Guide
American Quarterly
Annali Instituto Universitario Orientale (Napoli, Italy).
Antioch Review
Arts (France)
Atlantic

Ball State University Forum (formerly Ball State Teachers College Forum)
Best Sellers
Book World
Booklist
Bookmark
Bucknell Review
Bulletin of New York Public Library

Canadian Association for American Studies Bulletin
Canadian Forum
Catholic World
Chicago Review
Chicago Sun

Chicago Tribune
Choice
Christian Century
Christian Scholar's Review
Christian Science Monitor
Cleveland Open Shelf
Coastlines
College English
College Languages Association Journal
Comment: A New Zealand Quarterly Review
Commentary
Commonweal
Comparative Drama
Comparative Literature Studies
Conradiana
Contrast
Cosmopolitan
Cresset
Critical Quarterly
Critical Review (formerly Melbourne Critical Review)
Criticism

Dalhousie Review
Delta (Canada)
Drama (England)
Drama Criticism
Drama Critique

Drama Survey

Economist
Educational Theatre Journal
Emory University Quarterly
Encore (London, England)
Encounter
English Journal
English Miscellany (Delhi)
English Record
English Studies
Esquire

Film Quarterly
Folio (Indiana University)
Fortune
Forum

Harper's
Harper's Bazaar
Hibbert Journal
Holiday
House and Garden
Hudson Review

Illinois Quarterly
Illustrated London News (London, England)
Indian Essays (India)
Inostrannaya Literature
Insight

Jewish Quarterly
Journal of Aesthetics and Art Criticism
Journal of American Studies
Journal of Counseling Psychology

Kirkus

Library Journal
Life
Listener
Literary Half-Yearly
Lock Haven Review
London Magazine (London, England)

Look
Lugano Review

McCalls
McNeese Review
Manchester Guardian (England)
Melbourne Critical Review (see Critical Review)
Michigan Quarterly Review
Modern Drama
Modern Photography
Modern Review
Modern Sprak (Sweden)
Monthly Catalog
Musician

Nation
National Review
New England Quarterly
New Haven Register
New Hungarian Quarterly
New Leader
New Republic
New Statesman (formerly New Statesman and Nation)
New York Daily News
New York Herald Tribune
New York Journal-American
New York Post
New York Review of Books
New York Sun
New York Theatre Critics' Reviews
New York Times
New York World-Telegram
New Yorker
Newsweek
Notes & Queries (England)
Notes on Contemporary Literature

Observer
Ohio Review

Panjab University Research Bulletin (Pakistan)
Paris Review
Partisan Review

Perspectives
Personalist
Players Magazine
Popular Science
Prairie Schooner
Psychoanalytic Review
Publishers Weekly

Quarterly Journal of Speech
Quest

Ramparts
Re: Arts and Letters
Redbook
Renascence
Reporter
Revue des Langues Vivantes
  (Belgium)
Revue Nouvelle (Belgium)

San Francisco Chronicle
Saturday Evening Post
Saturday Review of Litera-
  ture
Saturday Review/World (for-
  merly Saturday Review)
Scholastic
School and Society
Scrif
Sewanee Review
Shenandoah
Sixties
South Atlantic Quarterly
Southern Humanities Review
Southern Review
Spectator
Springfield Republican
Sunday Times (London, Eng-
  land)

Tamarack Review
Theatre (Lincoln Center,
  New York)
Theatre Annual
Theatre Arts
Theatre World
Time

Time and Tide
Times (England)
Times (London) Literary Sup-
  plement (England)
Transactions of the Wisconsin
  Academy of Sciences, Arts
  and Letters
Transatlantic Review
Tri-Quarterly
Tulane Drama Review
Twentieth Century
Twentieth Century Literature

U.S. News and World Report
Universities and Left Review
University College Quarterly
University of Denver Quarterly
University of Texas Studies in
  Literature and Language
University of Toronto Quarterly

Virginia Quarterly Review
Vogue

Washington Post and Times
  Herald
Western Humanities Review
Western Review
Western Speech
Wisconsin Library Bulletin
Wisconsin Studies in Contem-
  porary Literature
World Theatre

Xavier University Studies
  (Louisiana)

Yale Literary Magazine
Yale Review

APPENDIX III

ARTHUR MILLER'S UNPUBLISHED MANUSCRIPTS,
LETTERS, AND POSTCARDS

[The listing is made essentially in accordance with the checklist each institution prepared for the compiler. Use the "Key
to Abbreviations" whenever necessary.]

I. THE AMERICAN ACADEMY OF ARTS AND LETTERS
   633 West 155th Street
   New York, NY 10032

   The following letters are addressed to different officers
     of the National Institute of Arts and Letters concern-
     ing meetings, nominations, etc.
   TLS Feb. 6, 1958, to Felicia Geffen, 1 p.
   TLS April 3, 1958, to Malcolm Cowley.
   TLS Jan. 9, 1959, to Louise Bogan.
   TLS Jan. 14, 1959, to Louise Bogan.
   TLS Jan. 19, 1959, to Glenway Wescott.
   AP October, 1960.
   Nomination certificate of Arthur Miller for member-
     ship to the National Institute.
   Various newspaper clippings.

II. THE LIBRARY OF CONGRESS
    Washington, D.C. 20003

    The Four Freedoms (Unpublished Radio Play), 1942.
      Typescript in the Library of Congress.
    Listen My Children (Unpublished "Comedy Satire with
      Music"), by AM and Norman Rosten, 1939. Type-
      script in the Library of Congress.

III. NEW YORK PUBLIC LIBRARY
      5th Avenue and 42nd Street
      New York, N. Y. 10018

      Promptbook of The Price with stage directions, light
      and sound cues, and "Author's Production Note,"
      gift of Mr. M. and Robert Whitehead Productions;
      described as "a copy of the stage manager's working
      script of the Broadway production." Earlier Xerox
      typescript, copyright 1967, gift of Lee Sabinson.
      Xerox copy of letter to John Wharton, July 29, 1969,
      on the occasion of his 75th birthday. Gift of Hobe
      Morrison.
      Letter signed "Arthur" to Cheryl Crawford, 16 Sept.,
      1958, re A Memory of Two Mondays, etc.
      They Too Arise. (1938) (MS.).

IV. THE UNIVERSITY OF MICHIGAN

     A. THE HOPWOOD ROOM
        1006 Angell Hall
        Ann Arbor, Michigan 48104

        Honors at Dawn, 1937, 98 pp. Typescript. Winner
           of Hopwood Minor Award in Drama, 1937.
        No Villain, 1936, 60 pp. Typescript. Winner of
           Hopwood Minor Award in Drama, 1936. Another
           version of this play was produced under the title
           They Too Arise, by the Hillel players in Lydia
           Mendelssohn Theatre, Ann Arbor, March 12-13,
           1937.
        "On Recognition" [1963], 17 pp. Typescript (carbon
           copy). The Hopwood lecture, 1963. Published
           in Michigan Quarterly Review, Oct., 1963.
        Decision of judge, Hopwood contest, 1948. Two
           printed forms completed in holograph, and signed.
        ALS Dec. 15, 1947 to Roy W. Cowden.
        TLS Feb. 22, 1948 to Roy W. Cowden.
        ANS Apr. 28, 1948 to Roy W. Cowden. Post card.
        TLS Apr. 29, 1948 to Roy W. Cowden. Post script
           in holograph. 2 enclosures.
        TLS [May 2?, 1948] to Roy W. Cowden.
        TLS Jan. 16, 1954 to Arno L. Bader.
        ALS Oct. 24, 1962 to Arno L. Bader. With enve-
           lope.
        ANS Nov. 2, 19[63?] to Hopwood Room. Post card.
        ALS Apr. 15, 1965 to Arno L. Bader.

B. THE UNIVERSITY OF MICHIGAN LIBRARY
Department of Rare Books and Special Collections

The Grass Still Grows, 1939, 143 pp. Typescript
(carbon copy) signed. A play in 3 acts. Manuscript notation on title page: Revised 3-6-39. A
rewritten version of No Villain.
Untitled play [1938?], 108 pp. Typescript (carbon
copy) signed. A play in 3 acts. With holograph
and typescript revisions. Referred to as "the
Jackson Prison play" because it grew out of a
visit to Jackson State Prison. Never published,
never produced.
TLS Nov. 13, 1965 to Chloe Aaron.
TLS [May ? 1967] to H. C. Jameson.
TLS Aug. 18, 1967 to H. C. Jameson.
TLS Jan. 25, 1968 to H. C. Jameson.

C. OFFICE OF THE PRESIDENT

"The Lines Between the Lines" [1965?] Published in
Our Michigan, edited by Erich A. Walter. Ann
Arbor, The University of Michigan, 1966, pp. 119-
22.
Correspondence concerning the granting of an honor-
ary degree (L. H. D.) in 1956.

V.   THE UNIVERSITY OF TEXAS LIBRARY
[Arthur Miller Manuscripts deposited in the Univ. of
Texas Library, Austin, Texas 78712]

MANUSCRIPTS:

(1) [After the Fall]. MS early working draft with many
suggestions for title throughout (33 pp.), January
27, 1958 (included within The Misfits. 2 AMS
notebooks. n. d.).
(2) [All My Sons]. Ams working notebook. n. d.
All My Sons. Mimeographed with ANS by Miller on
title page. July 14, 1947.
All My Sons. Tms, T/cc ms., and mimeographed/
printer's copy with ANS by Miller on title page.
n. d.
[All My Sons]. Tr. into the Italian: Tutti eiei figli.
T/cc ms with ANS by Miller on title page [1947]
All My Sons (The Sign of the Archer). T/cc ms

with Miller's note: "early version of All My Sons," n. d.

See The Sign of the Archer.

(3) Collected Plays (Introduction). Tms/inc "discarded" version with A revisions, n. d.

Collected Plays (Introduction). Tms with A revisions, n. d.

Collected Plays (Introduction). Tms with A revisions, n. d.

(4) Concerning the Boom. T/cc ms/ final. n. d.

Concerning the Boom. Tms S. n. d.

(5) [The Crucible]. Ams notebook. n. d. Title on cover: Those familiar spirits II.

[The Crucible]. Ams notebook. n. d.

The Crucible. T/cc ms with few A revisions and with ANS by Miller on title page. n. d.

The Crucible. Tms/final revised script. n. d.

[The Crucible]. Tms/first typed draft with extensive A revisions. September 11, 1952.

The Crucible. Tms S/first version with ANS by Miller on title page. n. d.

The Crucible: Act I, Scene I and II. Tms with A revisions. n. d.

[The Crucible]. inc. Tms/misc pp of different versions with many A revisions. n. d.

The Crucible: Act 1, Scene II. T/cc with ANS by Kermit Bloomgarden attached: "Copy used by Hart Stenographic." Nov. 22, 1952.

The Crucible: Act I, Scene I. T/cc ms with ANS by Kermit attached: "Copy used by Anne Meyerson." Nov. 22, 1952.

The Crucible: Act I, Scenes I and II. Tms and T/cc ms final revision with A revisions. Nov. 22, 1952.

The Crucible: Act II. Scene I. Tms with A revisions. n. d.

[The Crucible]. Adaptation cinematographique by Jean-Paul Sartre. Mimeographed with ANS on title page by Miller. n. d.

[The Crucible]. Adapted and translated into the French by Marcel Ayme. Mimeographed with ANS by Miller on first page. n. d.

[The Crucible]. inc. scenes from Les Sorcieres de Salem by Sartre. Mimeographed with 2 ANS by Miller. n. d.

The Crucible. Jean-Paul Sartre, "La Chasse aux Sorcieres" (prologue). Mimeographed with ANS

by Miller on first page. n. d. (See Les Sorcieres
de Salem.)
(6) Death of a Salesman. AMS notebook. n. d. Also
    in notebook: A View from the Bridge. A notes.
    Death of a Salesman. T/cc ms/ final script with A
    revisions and ANS by Miller on first page. n. d.
    Death of a Salesman. T/cc ms/ second version.
    n. d.
    Death of a Salesman. "In Memorium," Tms/ photo-
    stat of a story which became Death of a Sales-
    man with ANS by Miller attached. c. 1932.
    Death of a Salesman. Mimeographed/final draft with
    ANS by Miller on title page. August 3, 1951.
    Death of a Salesman. Mimeographed with ANS by
    Miller on title page. n. d.
    Death of a Salesman. Translated into the Spanish.
    Mimeographed with ANS by Miller on title page.
    n. d. (See A View from the Bridge. See "In
    Memorium. ")
(7) Focus. Tms and T/cc ms/pp from intermediate
    draft with A revision. n. d.
    Focus. Tms with many A revisions. n. d.
    Focus. Some shall not sleep. T/cc ms/ early
    draft with additions and emendations (246 pp.
    with pp. 175-85 missing). n. d.
(8) Forbidden Vision (the original title of I Don't Need
    You Anymore) (see I Don't Need You Anymore).
(9) From Under the Sea, a play in one act (the original
    title of A View from the Bridge), (1955).
(10) [The Golden Years]. Act I: Scene I and II. T/cc
    ms. n. d.
    The Golden Years. T/cc ms. (108 pp.) C. 1939.
    Unpublished.
    The Golden Years. T/cc msS with his ANS on title
    page. 1939-1940.
(11) [The Grass Still Grows]. T/cc ms with A revisions
    and his ANS on title page. 1935. Original title:
    They Too Arise.
    The Grass Still Grows. TmsS. n. d. Revision of
    They Too Arise.
    The Grass Still Grows. T/cc ms with his ANS on
    title page. June 8, 1939 (second revision of
    They Too Arise) (see They Too Arise).
(12) The Half-Bridge: A Play in Three Acts. Tms and
    T/cc msS with his ANS on title page. 1941-1943.
(13) The Hook. Ams notebook. n. d.
    The Hook: A Play for the Screen. T/cc msS with

his ANS on title page. 1951. Included with this
is Tms/fragments for shooting script (6 pp.)
The Grass Still Grows (Unpublished Revision of They
Too Arise), 1939. Typescript in the Academic
Center Library, University of Texas.
The Half-Bridge (Unpublished Play), 1941-43. Typescript in the Academic Center Library, University of Texas.
The Hook (Unpublished Screenplay), 1951. Typescript in the Academic Center Library, University of Texas.
(14) [I Don't Need You Anymore]. 5 Tms and Tcc/ms/
early version/inc with many A revisions. n.d.
[I Don't Need You Anymore]. Tms/first/draft/inc
with A revisions. n.d. (Revision of Forbidden
Vision).
[I Don't Need You Anymore]. 12 Tms and T/cc
ms/inc versions with A revisions. n.d.
[I Don't Need You Anymore]. 12 Tms and T/cc
ms/inc versions with A revisions. n.d.
[I Don't Need You Anymore]. T/cc ms/pp, 1-39.
n.d.
I Don't Need You Anymore. Tms with many A revisions. March 17, 1959. (See Forbidden Vision.)
(15) "In Memorium." Tms/photostat of story which be-
came Death of a Salesman with ANS by Miller
attached c. 1932 (see Death of a Salesman).
"In Memorium" (Unpublished short story), c. 1932
Typescript in the Academic Center Library, University of Texas (listed as the "story which be-
came Death of a Salesman").
(16) Joe the Motorman. Tms with ANS by Miller on
first page. n.d.
(17) The Man Who Had All the Luck. T/cc ms/ Stage
manager's copy with some A notes in Miller's
hand. n.d.
The Man Who Had All the Luck. T/cc ms with 4
Ams pp. inserted. n.d.
The Man Who Had All the Luck: A Play in 3 Acts.
T/cc ms with ANS by Miller on title page. n.d.
The Man Who Had All the Luck: Something Like a
Fable. Tms with A revisions. n.d.
(18) A Memory of Two Mondays. Mimeographed/
printer's copy with ANS by Miller. n.d.
A Memory of Two Mondays. Mimeographed with A
revisions and T inserts. n.d.

A Memory of Two Mondays: An Improvisation on a
Bygone Year. Mimeographed with A revisions
and one T p. inserted. n. d.
A Memory of Two Mondays: An Improvisation on a
Bygone Year. Tms with A revisions. n. d.
A Memory of Two Mondays: A Play in One Act.
Tms with extensive A revisions. n. d.
(19) [The Misfits.] Tms fragment with A emendations,
5 pp. n. d. Intermediary workings that follow the
screenplay and precede the cinema novel. Included with this: T/ccms fragment with A emendations. 7 pp. n. d. Composed later intermediary material.
The Misfits. (N. B.: This version has many pages
missing (probably rejected), many pages that are
deleted (as though to be rejected), and several inserts which are on a different kind of paper).
The Misfits. Tms and Tccms (second) draft of cinema novel version with A emendations (168 pp).
(Revision...September 1959) Date deleted: June
15, 1959.
The Misfits. T mimeo (third) draft of cinema novel
version with A emendations (167 pp.)
The Misfits. 2 Ams notebooks, 119 pp. n. d. Included within this: (After the Fall), Ams early
working draft, 33 pp. January 27, 1958.
[The Misfits]. The (first) draft/inc. of cinema novel version with A emendation. 36 pp. n. d.
The Misfits. Tms (second) draft with A emendations. 149 pp. October, 1957. This version
labeled "1st draft...October 1957."
The Misfits. Tms (third) draft with A emendations
and ANS by Miller on title page. 165 pp. "First
draft, October 28, 1957." Bound.
The Misfits. Tms (fourth) draft with A emendations
and insertions. 115 pp. "First draft October 28,
1947" (Typographical error; should be October 28,
1957).
The Misfits. T mimeo (fourth) draft of cinema novel version with Tms inserts and A emendations
(199 pp.) "Revision...March 1960."
[The Misfits]. Composite Tms, Tccms, T mimeo.,
and T thermofax/Movie version with extensive revisions. 236 p. July 13, 1960-October 22, 1960.
Signed in several places. Bound.
[The Misfits]. Tms (first draft/inc with A emendations. 116 pp. n. d.

[The Misfits]. Ams fragment ending of cinema novel version 2 pp. n. d.

[The Misfits]. Tms fragment of cinema novel version with A emendations. 2 pp. n. d.

[The Misfits: Rejected pp. I]. Tms fragments with A emendations (N.B.: Mss paginated by cataloger).

[The Misfits: Final Rejects for Viking version]. Tms fragments with A emendations. 30 pp. n. d.

[The Misfits: Rejected pp. III]. Tms fragments with A emendations. 35 pp. n. d. (N.B.: Mss paginated by cataloger).

[The Misfits: Rejected pp. II]. Tms fragments with A emendations (N.B.: Mss paginated by cataloger).

(20) One of the Brooklyn Villages (Autobiographical sketch). TmsS with A and T emendations. 18 pp. n. d.

(21) [A Peek into the Future]. T/cc ms/ "published in The Nation." n. d.
A Peek into the Future. Tms/first draft with A revisions. n. d.

(22) Please Don't Kill Anything. Tms with A revisions.
Please Don't Kill Anything. T/cc ms with A revisions. n. d.

(23) The Role of Men of the Mind in the World Today. Tms with A revisions. 1960.

(24) The Sign of the Archer. T/cc ms with Miller's note: "Early version of All My Sons." n. d. (see All My Sons).

(25) Social Plays: What Are They? (Introduction to A View from the Bridge). Tms with extensive A revisions. n. d. (see A View from the Bridge.)

(26) Les Socieres de Salem by Jean-Paul Sartre (adaptation of The Crucible) (see The Crucible).

(27) Speech to New Dramatists Committee. Tms with A revisions. c. 1956-1957.

(28) They Too Arise (the original title of The Grass Still Grows).

(29) Two Years. Tms with Ans by Miller, n. d.

(30) The University of Michigan. TmsS with A revisions. n. d.

(31) [A View from the Bridge]. Tms with extensive A revisions with ANS on title page. Feb. 28, 1955.
First title: From Under the Sea.
A View from the Bridge. A notes. n. d. Written in Ams notebook: Death of a Salesman.

[A View from the Bridge]. Mimeographed/early
  version with 20 pp. of Tms inserted. n.d.
A View from the Bridge. Mimeographed with ANS
  from Miller to Kay Brown. Mimeographed inserts for British version. n.d.
[A View from the Bridge]. Mimeographed with Mil-
  ler's A notes on actors' performances and A re-
  visions. n.d.
A View from the Bridge. Motion picture script by
  Norman Rosten. T/cc ms with ANS by Miller on
  title page. n.d.
A View from the Bridge. Printer's copy/pp. 74-
  155. Mimeographed with ANS by Miller on title
  page. n.d.
A View from the Bridge. Tr. into the French by
  Marcel Ayme. Mimeographed with T/cc ms. in-
  serts and ANS by Miller on title page. n.d.
A View from the Bridge. Tms with A revisions.
  Feb. 28, 1955.
A View from the Bridge. Social Plays: What Are
  They? (Introduction to A View from the Bridge).
  Tms with extensive A revisions. n.d. (see
  From Under the Sea; Death of a Salesman; and
  Social Plays: What Are They?).
(32) William Ireland's Confession. TmsS/cut version of
  published play. January 5, 1944.
William Ireland's Confession: A Historical Play.
  T/cc ms with ANS by Miller on first page. n.d.
LETTERS:

ALS to Mrs. Dean. n.d.
ANS (no recipient known). March 1958. Written on:
  TLS from Micheline Rozan to Kay Brown.
TLS (by secretary) to Robert Spira. January 23, 1957
  (Reg. #1444).
TLS to Dame Edith Sitwell. May 24, 1957.
TLS to Arthur Miller. Christian Science Monitor.
  Feb. 9, 1956.

REPORTS:

Wilminson, Richard Thomas. Arthur Miller Manuscripts at the University of Texas. TMS (report).

THE UNIVERSITY OF TEXAS HUMANITIES RESEARCH
CENTER LIBRARY added the following after 1967:

Address to PEN Congress, New York, June 1966.
Typed ms., signed, with revisions [7pp.]
Interview with Ronald Hayman. Typed ms. with revisions [20 pp.] undated.
Fame [play] Typed first draft, signed, with revisions [12 pp.] dated May 1969. Typed final draft, signed, with emendations [14 pp.] undated.

VI. THE VIKING PRESS, INC.
625 Madison Avenue
New York, N.Y. 10022

Letters by Miller to Pascal Covici: TL 1949-1964.
Letters to Mr. Thomas H. Guinzburg, President.

INDEX